STRENGTHENING CONGRESS

STRENGTHENING CONGRESS

Lee H. Hamilton

Indiana University Press

BLOOMINGTON AND INDIANAPOLIS

This book is a publication of
INDIANA UNIVERSITY PRESS
601 North Morton Street
Bloomington, IN 47404-3797 USA

www.iupress.indiana.edu

Telephone orders 800-842-6796
Fax orders 812-855-7931
Orders by e-mail iuporder@indiana.edu

Library of Congress Cataloging-in-Publication Data

Hamilton, Lee.
   Strengthening Congress / Lee H. Hamilton.
      p.   cm.
   Includes bibliographical references and index.
   ISBN 978-0-253-30032-4 (cl : alk. paper) — ISBN 978-0-253-22165-0 (pbk : alk. paper) 1. United States. Congress. I. Title.
   JK1021.H363 2009
   328.73—dc22

                                                    2009012459

      1   2   3   4   5   14   13   12   11   10   09

Contents

Preface

This is a book about belief in the face of cynicism. Americans have a deeply jaundiced view of Congress at the moment, and as you'll see in the pages that follow, there's often good reason for this. Yet for over two centuries, Congress has stood at the heart of the American experiment: giving in to disenchantment without exploring remedies would mean forsaking the principles our democracy was founded upon. At this moment in our history, we need to talk about how to strengthen Congress, not just about the ways it disappoints us.

Having served on Capitol Hill for thirty-four years, I've come to believe profoundly in our representative democracy—in the notion that the representatives of a diverse and often divided people can come together to find common ground and solutions to the issues that confront us. That is what Congress is for, and why it is indispensable. If it is weakened, then we cannot hope to achieve what our Founders intended and Abraham Lincoln articulated: government of, by, and for the people.

And Congress today *is* weak. Many Americans believe it has little relevance to their lives, are uninterested in its work, and see no reason to engage with their House members or senators. Presidents over the last few decades have worked hard to arrogate to themselves its powers and responsibilities. And far too often, Congress has seemed uninterested in pushing back or in standing up for its institutional integrity. In all this, it falls far short of the role envisioned for it by the Founders.

I don't believe this can continue if we hope to retain our representative democracy. There is no guarantee in the Constitution that our system will endure without careful tending—as John F. Kennedy put it, "Democracy is never a final achievement." Every American has an interest in seeing our most accessible and representative institution of government improve, since a robust and vibrant representative government depends on having a presidency and a Congress that are the equal of each other in strength. As this is written, we are in the early stages of a new presidential administration that many Americans hope will restore their faith in the federal government. Yet I would argue that, without a vigorous Congress, our government simply will not function as well as Americans would like.

In the end, this is a matter of political will. It has not been at all clear in recent years that members of Congress as a whole are interested in playing the assertive role the Constitution foresees for them. In this book, I lay out some ideas for how they—and you—can work to buttress what has come to be called "the broken branch." It is an attempt to be constructive at a time of great opportunity, and though I would not expect every reader to agree with all the proposals I put forward, perhaps all would agree that making Congress a stronger institution is an important step toward creating a more perfect union.

This book grew out of my series of biweekly commentaries on Congress. These cover a wide range of topics related to Congress, but in recent years I found I was increasingly coming back to the central theme of the need to strengthen the institution I served in and still deeply admire. In an earlier book, *How Congress Works and Why You Should Care,* I focused mostly on understanding Congress; this volume moves forward a step to take a hard look at how the institution can better live up to its potential.

I would like to thank Rob Gurwitt and Ken Nelson for their talented help on the original commentaries and in expanding them to create this book. I am indebted to Ted Carmines, Phil Duncan, and Don Wolfensberger for their insightful comments as we pulled this book together.

I would also like to thank Laura Kunz for her assistance with the endnotes and her careful review of the manuscript, and Janet Rabinowitch of Indiana University Press for her encouragement and valuable support for this project. The royalties from the sale of this book will go to the Center on Congress at Indiana University, which has as its central mission to help ordinary citizens understand the crucial importance of the Congress in a representative democracy.

STRENGTHENING CONGRESS

1

Why We Need to Restore Power to Congress

WE FREQUENTLY see surveys of what Americans think are important challenges facing the country. Their concerns typically include keeping America safe, shoring up the economy, and protecting individual liberties. These are all significant, yet there is one item you can be certain will not be on this list: strengthening Congress. It ought to be.

Why does it belong there? Congress was set up as the "first branch" in our system of government, but it has seen its powers erode significantly over the years, especially in recent decades; its relative stature at the moment would be an unpleasant surprise to James Madison and the other Founders. Whether Congress reasserts itself and lives up to its constitutional responsibilities isn't just a matter for academics to discuss. It matters deeply to all of us.

The Intent of the Founders

Halfway through George W. Bush's presidency, Vice President Dick Cheney appeared on the History Channel to reflect on the administration's drive to centralize and expand White House power in Washington. The presidency, he argued, had been hemmed in after the Vietnam War and Watergate, and it had taken years of effort to return it to its rightful prerogatives. "I think there has been over time a restoration, if you will, of the power and authority of the president," he said, and went on to suggest that this was just and proper.[1]

I was struck by his comments, because though the former vice president and I have served in public life over much the same period of time, we have come to opposite conclusions. It was a deeply felt conviction within the Bush administration, and other administrations as well, that the presidency had to be protected and strengthened; the Bush White House frequently approached national policy from that premise. I believe that the nation benefits from a strong presidency, and I would not want to see that office weakened. Yet I've also come to believe that to make democracy work, presidential power must be checked and balanced by an equally strong Congress. To me, the problem is not that the presidency is too hemmed in, but that Congress in recent times has become too weak and timid. The president is now the de facto chief legislator—he sets the policy agenda and is by far the most dominant player in establishing the federal budget. If power needs bolstering anywhere in Washington, it's on Capitol Hill.

I'll admit that the course of American history throughout the twentieth century and into the twenty-first has upheld Vice President Cheney's side, as a series of presidents have worked to bulk up White House power. On my side, though, I've got the Founders. With the exception of Alexander Hamilton, they wanted Congress to be the engine of policy and of law in the United States. They devoted the first article of the Constitution to enumerating its powers, and spent most of their time at the Constitutional Convention of 1787 arguing over its shape and reach.

The reasons are straightforward. In part, they were worried about the concentration of power: in the hands of a single person, of a few people, or even of a majority. That is what our system's "checks and balances" were designed to thwart. But they also believed that in a representative democracy, in which "the people are the only legitimate fountain of power," as James Madison put it, Congress was the avenue through which the American people would express their wishes.[2] It was inconceivable to them that a single chief executive could represent the priorities and desires of a diverse nation.

They were right. As power shifts from Congress to the president and the executive branch, the federal government inevitably becomes less representative. For all their faults, members of Congress understand their constituents exceedingly well. The president cannot possibly grasp their concerns as intimately or represent as directly the needs of 300 million Americans.

Congress, at its best, brings great strength to the system. The White House and executive agencies are far less accessible to ordinary voters than Congress is, and while I am well aware that Congress can be too easily swayed by powerful or monied interests, at least ordinary citizens have a chance to engage their representatives if they want. When was the last time you went to a community supper with the secretary of defense?

Similarly, the White House cannot reflect the diversity of the American people. It is on Capitol Hill that the regional, class, social, ideological, racial, and ethnic variety of this nation's residents is manifested and, more important, where it must be taken into account. It is hard work to reconcile the diverse interests that come into play around a particular issue, but that is what Congress is for, and efforts to bypass it in the name of efficiency and speed are in reality little more than shrugging off the democratic process.

Finally, when Congress loses power, the nation loses accountability and transparency in the policy-making process. The executive branch is not open to public view. Congress is—or at least it ought to be. When Congress behaves timidly, the strongest muscle Americans have for getting at the roots of problems—the congressional oversight process—never gets flexed. The field is left open for the White House to put its own spin on public policy.

There is, I must acknowledge, a weak spot in my view. It is that the Congress sometimes cannot get its act together well enough to be a strong, effective, and sustained counterbalance to the power of the presidency. That is why reforming the Congress, as difficult as that may be, is crucial. Until this happens, the power of the presidency will continue to grow.

I understand the pressures that have led us here: wars and terrorism inevitably call for the exercise of presidential power; chief executives quite naturally place a high value on their own agendas; the complexity of the legislative process makes Congress seem a burdensome part of the policy-making process; and the very diversity that underlies Congress's legitimacy also undercuts its ability to speak with one voice. Yet I remain puzzled by the willingness of the Congress itself to yield power, as it has done when it comes to declaring war. True, Democrats and Republicans both like to bolster presidents of their own party, but they also have a responsibility under the Constitution to ensure that their own institution is at least an equal with the presidency in governing the country.

Indeed, they may not remember it, but they've actually taken an oath to that effect. When a member of Congress is sworn in, he or she vows to support and defend the Constitution, a document that right up top says that "all legislative powers herein granted shall be vested" in Congress. It hardly seems a radical step, or even disrespectful of the presidency, for Congress to turn itself into an equal partner and start behaving as if it took those words seriously.

Ceding Responsibilities to the President

To the casual observer, Congress can seem unusually pushy—tussling with the White House over the budget, investigating executive agency shortcomings, expanding the number of oversight hearings. Many Americans, who don't much like out-and-out conflict among their political leaders, find themselves wondering whether those politicians on Capitol Hill are going a little overboard.

The short answer is no. Not even close.

This is not a partisan comment about Democrats and Republicans. It's about the relationship between Capitol Hill and the White House, and how important it is to our system that each—the presidency and the Congress—be a strong and vibrant institution.

What the framers of our Constitution sought above all was balance: between large states and small, minority rights and majority rule, executive power and legislative authority. To keep the president from becoming too powerful, they not only created an equally powerful Congress, they explicitly gave it authority to declare war, to enact taxes, and to set the budgetary agenda. They wanted to ensure that consultation, debate, and the voices of the American people would all have a prominent place in the halls of power. Yet they did not want an unchecked Congress either. They believed that the interaction between two powerful branches of government would be broadly responsive to the people, and the balance between each branch would produce more authoritative and better policy.

Yet over the last several decades, on issue after issue, Congress has slowly but inexorably ceded its constitutionally mandated responsibilities to the president. Presidents of both parties have sought and encouraged this trend, although it accelerated under President Bush, who pursued a definition of executive power more all-encompassing than that of any of his immediate predecessors. Congress also faces some loss of power to judicial activism, encroachment by the courts in areas traditionally handled by Congress; yet this has not been nearly as extensive as the loss to presidential encroachment.

Perhaps the most vivid example of this overall shift in power lies in the weightiest decision a government has to make: whether to go to war against another country. The Constitution unequivocally grants this authority to Congress, and it does so for a reason: our founders did not want the decision to be made by one person, but by many. In case after case since the Korean conflict, however, Congress has essentially handed off war-making power to the president, and presidents have been only too eager to accept it. The constitutional injunction—that the Congress shall have the power to declare war—has basically become a nullity. In the popular mind as well as in practice, war has become a presidential prerogative.

Similarly, Congress has over the last few decades grown increasingly sluggish when it comes to budgeting—that is, creating the basic blueprint for what our government will do by means of thousands of federal programs, large and small. Not only has it ceded the initiative to the president, who submits the budget to which Congress merely responds, it has repeatedly failed to come up with its own clear vision for government spending; year after year, the president determines the vast majority of the federal budget, while Congress gets to tinker on the margins. And only four times in the last thirty years has Congress passed all its appropriations bills on time.[3] This has forced budgetary decisions into massive omnibus bills, allowing presidents to negotiate with only a handful of congressional leaders—not committee chairs—and making the threat of a veto far more potent.

War and the budget are not the only arenas in which Congress has reduced its role. It is the president who basically sets the agenda for which major issues Congress will take up each year. On everything from the fight against terrorism to international trade to environmental protection, the president and the executive branch have become the driving forces in American governance. Congress, though not entirely supine, has been content to let the president take the political heat for actually leading. When he was president, George Washington made only a few suggestions for legislation, and refrained from commenting on matters before Congress. President Washington would not recognize how we do things today.

While Congress has been handing more power over to the president, it has not at the same time increased its oversight to make sure that power is being used effectively and properly. A *Washington Post* editor recently put it succinctly: "Congress has become less vigilant, less proud and protective of its own prerogatives, and less important to the conduct of American government than at any time in decades."[4]

To be sure, the world our nation faces is vastly different from the one the Framers confronted or could even envision in 1789. In a difficult world, an increase in presidential power is appropriate. But a weak Congress is not. A Congress that reasserts its prerogatives as a co-equal branch of government, that insists on robust oversight of the executive branch, that sets its own agenda as well as responds to the agenda of the president, that exercises the powers given it by our Constitution when it comes to declaring war and deciding how the government will spend its money—this would not be a Congress that weakens the president, but rather one that strengthens our democracy.

Why Does Congress Want to Give up Power?

Politicians like power. The more they have, the better they can set public agendas, create policy, help their constituents, and affect the direction of government.

Members of Congress like power just as much as you'd expect of people holding high federal office. That's why they want to gain seniority on their committees, jockey for assignments to powerful committees, and rise in the leadership. If they're in the House of Representatives, they often have their eye on the Senate. If they're in the Senate, they can't help but glance over at a governorship or the White House. This is the nature of the office.

Yet it gives rise to one of the more perplexing and important mysteries of life in Washington right now: Why, if they hunger after power, have members of Congress been so willing to hand it off to the executive branch? Why have they been willing over the last three or four decades to weaken Congress as an institution?

For while many members over the years have sought individual power on Capitol Hill, they have seemed to fall over one another to give Congress's power to the president and his cabinet, or to countenance executive-branch reaches for power. They have effectively ceded to the president the ability to declare war, a responsibility the Constitution unambiguously lays on Congress's shoulders. They have largely handed to the White House the power to set their own legislative agenda. They have weakened their oversight of the executive branch, too often giving the president and administration officials unchecked authority to implement scores of laws without robust scrutiny. And every so often, they seriously entertain giving the president even more power of the purse—another responsibility vested in Congress by the Constitution—by granting the president an extensive line-item veto.

I can't pretend to understand this development fully. I watched it unfold during my three decades in the U.S. House of Representatives, and I've watched it accelerate since I left office in 1999, and it still perplexes me. Our nation's founders had good reasons for creating a system that balances an energetic executive branch with an equally forceful and powerful legislative branch. Why undo their work?

Part of the reason, I believe, is quite simply that times have changed. As complex as the affairs of state must have seemed in 1789, they are exponentially more complicated now. I fully understand Woodrow Wilson's claim that the presidency is "the vital place of action in the system."[5] Often the cumbersome separation of powers does not work in dealing with the challenges of the day, and the president needs to take the initiative. In addition, on issues from national security to, say, the safety of our food, there is only so much that can be accomplished by passing new legislation. Much of the hard work of carrying out public policy is in the implementation, which is the task of the president and the executive branch, not the Congress. So to some extent, members of Congress have had no choice but to allow a vigorous executive branch to stretch its wings.

Yet that does not entirely explain the timidity of Congress over the past few decades. There is more at play here than simply a change in the substantive nature of the federal workload. It is, in a word, politics.

Congress does not work smoothly. It can be difficult and time-consuming to develop a legislative consensus among 535 representatives and senators who have many competing interests and agendas. This means that Congress works in shades of gray and in long increments of time. Many members, as a result, wonder whether the Congress can be effective or efficient in dealing with the complex issues of the day. Members of Congress could give you a lot of other reasons why they have let slip their institution's responsibilities and best traditions: the need to tend to districts with 650,000 constituents; the constant need to raise money; their hectic schedules and the hundreds of votes they must cast each year. The list goes on and on. They have come to believe, perhaps because of the difficulty of legislating, that the president can do things better. Add to this the media's natural propensity to focus on the president—and, in this sound-bite era, to shy away from reporting on the complexities of congressional policy making—and you get a gradual loss of confidence in Congress.

At the same time, letting the president take the lead makes life much easier for members of Congress. When they are of the same party, the majority has a natural tendency to defer to the president's wishes. But even without that, taking a position on a difficult issue leaves a member of Congress politically exposed and complicates his or her next election. The far easier route is to delegate the tough decisions to the president; if they are handled well, you applaud, and if they are not, you condemn. Either way, you don't have to take political responsibility.

There is a severe cost to this, however, and it is measured in the erosion of the checks and balances and the constitutional structure envisioned by our founders. For our system to work, Congress needs to balance the president. And if it hands him any power with one hand, it needs to exert greater oversight with the other. That has not been happening. As a result, the people's body, the Congress, is a weakened institution, and is no longer playing the role of a separate and co-equal branch of government that our Founders envisioned.

What It Means When You Take That Oath of Office

Every member of Congress swears an oath at the beginning of each term to "support and defend" the Constitution. And while every member has to decide for himself or herself what this entails, I can't help but think that at least a few of the excesses we've seen in recent years on Capitol Hill might have been avoided if every member set aside a little time every so often to reflect on the meaning of that oath and why the Framers decided to have members swear allegiance to the Constitution.

To begin with, the Constitution asserts a profoundly democratic vision of this nation, a bedrock belief in the sovereignty of the people and a vision of how our structures of government are meant to secure freedom. The Preamble, with its sweeping talk of justice, promoting the general welfare, and securing "the blessings of liberty to ourselves and our posterity," is especially relevant here. Juxtapose this inspiring view of the hope underlying our system against the special favors some members have handed out to well-connected lobbyists, and it's not hard to see that more attention to the ideals of the Founders might have stood Congress in good stead.

But defending the Constitution is not just about giving life to the vision it lays out. That venerable document is also an operating manual for our government, and it strongly emphasizes the separation of powers. When you take the oath of office as a member of Congress, it means that you are swearing to defend the Congress as a strong, independent, and co-equal branch of government. Indeed, the longer one serves in Congress, the more loyalty one often develops to that body when it comes to sorting through the competing claims on its attention. A member's primary loyalty must go not to the president or his or her political party, but to the Constitution itself.

In fact, I would argue that the congressional oath of office requires members of Congress to protect the powers of Congress especially from encroachment by the executive branch. The Constitution certainly provides for a strong executive. "Energy in the executive," Alexander Hamilton once said, "is a leading character in the definition of good government," and he was right.[6] This does not mean, though, that Congress is free to ignore the careful balancing act embedded in the Constitution and allow its own prerogatives to be eroded. Vigor in the Congress is also, we might remember, a leading characteristic of good government. Better public policy emerges, believed the Founders, if both the president and the Congress are robust.

The administration of the oath of office is such a fleeting thing, a few quick words on the hectic opening day of each new Congress before its members dive into the hurly-burly of legislating, fighting partisan battles, and positioning themselves for the next election. It is easily overlooked. But we live in an era of a timid Congress and presidents who insist on strengthening their hand at the expense of Congress. At such a time, it seems to me, members of Congress need to take their oath of office seriously, and pay close attention to the Constitution they've sworn to protect and defend.

Our system of government is under some stress, but it is not fatally flawed. We do not need a new constitutional convention to right what is wrong with Congress. What needs to be fixed in the Congress demands no changes in the law. Congress simply needs to get its house in order and assert itself as a co-equal branch. Congress need only act as our founders intended it to.

2

A Stronger Voice

IF CONGRESS IS TO rebuild its institutional strength, its first order of business must be to learn how to articulate its sense of itself; it needs to regain its ability to speak with a strong voice. While there are any number of issues it might use to do this, the Constitution offers Congress three key policy arenas in which to exert itself: developing the federal budget, deciding to go to war, and setting the national agenda. Yet for decades now, the White House has taken the lead in all three.

Congress Should Do More than Tinker with the Budget

Often when it submits the federal budget to Congress in February, the White House proposes some measures to boost its own control over the budget process. It might suggest giving the president veto power over the annual congressional budget resolution—Congress's memo to itself on what it plans to do with federal spending—or creating a commission to review the performance of federal programs, a role that Congress is supposed to perform routinely. On Capitol Hill these measures are controversial, since legislators fret about handing too much budgetary power to the president. Their concern would be well-placed but for one thing: they've already done it.

True, you wouldn't think so if you'd listened to congressional leaders and committee chairmen over the past several years. They'll often maintain the pretense of congressional vitality by insisting that the White House's budget, or some significant portion of it, is "dead on arrival." They're fooling themselves. The president's budget sets the agenda, and every year the overwhelming majority of it—over 90 percent—gets enacted. This is true whether the president and the leaders of Congress are from the same party or different parties. Keep this in mind as you read about the wrangling over this or that program on Capitol Hill: it's largely tinkering. As a levelheaded insider's magazine, the *National Journal*, put it a few years ago, the president is "King of the Budget," and he'll get the vast majority of what he wants.[1]

Accustomed as we are to the president laying out the agenda for how the federal government ought to raise and spend the people's money, it's important to remember that for most of our nation's history it was different. The framers of the Constitution explicitly gave Congress, not the president, the authority to tax and spend. They rightly saw that "the power of the purse" is what sets the government on its course and allows it to function, and they wanted that power held by the "immediate representatives of the people," as James Madison put it. In fact, before 1921 the president didn't even prepare an overall budget proposal; instead, the various executive-branch agencies sent their requests for funding directly to Congress.

All of this began to change as the power of the presidency increased during the New Deal and World War II. More recently, however, what began as a rebalancing of budgetary initiative became a wholesale shift in power far beyond anything this nation had encountered before. If there is comprehensive debate over budgetary priorities these days, it takes place within the administration, as the various agencies and departments argue with the powerful Office of Management and Budget over their funding levels. Debate and votes within Congress, where the heart of our democracy is supposed to lie, often feel like an afterthought; at best, they affect the budget only on the margins. The Founders would be flabbergasted.

Some of this is due to changing budgetary circumstances. The "discretionary" portion of the budget—that is, the portion not given over to such entitlement programs as Social Security and Medicare, which are largely untouched by Congress—has shrunk over the years, to the point where it now makes up about a third of the budget. But that third includes spending on the military, which Congress is loath to touch, so in truth the room it leaves itself is even more limited than it appears.

The White House, too, has done what it could to chip away at congressional prerogatives. The George W. Bush administration, for example, acted forcefully to keep the Republican congressional leadership on the same page, and it excluded from the regular budget process some of the president's top priorities (such as funding the war in Iraq), which meant they received much less review than they would have otherwise.

But much of Congress's budgetary weakness is self-inflicted. It has failed in recent years to carry out robust oversight of federal programs, thereby depriving itself of a way to gauge their effectiveness at budget time. It has generally not taken up large issues—such as tax policy or health-care reform—independently of the president. And because it has been unable to finish on time the appropriations bills that lay out its own priorities, it has routinely passed continuing resolutions or omnibus bills rather than the carefully crafted budgets of a generation ago. The result is bad for the government and worse for the federal balance of power, since this expands the role of the president.

Putting together a budget is not glamorous work. It entails paying close attention to numbers, a mastery of obscure and often mind-numbing details about federal programs, and a willingness to spend long hours scrutinizing government in ways that are unlikely to garner much attention back home. Yet the budget is the basic operating document of the federal government. It was hardly an accident that when the Framers laid out the Congress's duties, the very first was "to lay and collect taxes . . . and provide for the common defense and general welfare of the United States." Few congressional responsibilities are more important.

The power of the purse given to Congress by the Constitution, in other words, is Capitol Hill's power to check the president's direction and suggest a different one. Clearly, the nation wants this. There is a growing recognition that Congress must in general reassert its authority. The budget is a key place to do so.

To be sure, Congress has made some progress toward cutting back on excessive "earmarks"—the expenditures on bridges, roads, museums, research programs, and other projects often derided as "pork"—and is to be commended for this. But eliminating an earmark doesn't eliminate the spending, only how it is allocated. Against the backdrop of Congress's far more costly habit of passing unaffordable entitlement spending and equally unaffordable tax cuts, it's only the tiniest of steps.

No Congress that really cared about fiscal responsibility would agree to raise spending and cut revenues as Congress habitually did even before the economic crisis that began late in 2007. Our current deficits are unsustainable. They threaten us with potentially crippling dependence on other countries, and impose heavy bills for current spending on our children and grandchildren. Yet when Congress focuses on reform, it tends to look at questions of process: Should it cap spending on Medicare? Should it change to a biennial budget cycle? Should it give the president a line-item veto or expand his rescission authority? Should it return to its "pay as you go" rules, mainly in effect during the Clinton years, which required it to find the money for spending proposals?

While some of these may be helpful—the recently re-adopted "pay-go" rules do, indeed, impose a measure of fiscal discipline on Congress—the truth is that none of them produces sound fiscal and budgetary policy, and some give even more power to the president.

The fundamental money issues facing Congress don't have to do with process, they have to do with hard choices. Simply put, Congress has to make sound fiscal decisions.

Why does this matter? Partly, of course, it's the issue itself. The budget is not now, and has not been for years, in fundamental balance. Just as important, getting control of the budget and behaving like the fiscal stewards our founders envisioned is the first step Congress must take if it is to be a co-equal branch of government. As long as it allows the power of the purse to lie elsewhere and pretends it's just along for the ride, Congress's claim to independence will ring hollow.

The Decision to Go to War

As Congress struggled to stave off the nation's financial meltdown in the fall of 2008, it was hard to imagine that it could ever face a more serious issue. Yet from time to time it does: when it ponders whether or not to send young Americans to war. Watching the gyrations on Capitol Hill over the economic bailout, I couldn't help but reflect that while there was great uncertainty about how Congress would respond to the economic crisis—Would it side with the White House plan? Would it modify the plan or try to come up with an alternative of its own?—there is rarely uncertainty about war. If the president wants it, he gets it.

Our nation has long argued over whether this is how things should be. To my mind, the Constitution seems clear on the subject, stating in Article I, Section 8, that "Congress shall have power . . . to declare War." Yet it also refers to the president as "Commander in Chief," and the ambiguity left by those two phrases has seeded an ongoing political debate over how much right Congress has to tie the president's hands when it comes to the commitment of troops abroad. The courts, recognizing a political morass, have steered clear of the subject, leaving it to Congress and the White House to sort things out, and by and large not settling the question of which branch may exercise which powers.

Since World War II, the White House has prevailed. Harry Truman contended he didn't need congressional approval to fight in Korea. Congress sat on the sidelines for the invasions of Panama and Grenada in the 1980s, and made only modest steps to assert itself when U.S. troops got involved in Somalia in 1992, Haiti in 1994, and the Balkans in the mid-1990s. It willingly gave its go-ahead to the Vietnam War and the two wars in Iraq, basically turning power over to the president to do as he wished. In essence, for over a half century Congress has been content to act as a postscript when it comes to war making, rather than as the president's equal. It has left the question of when to go to war up to the president.

The political reasons for this abdication of responsibility are straightforward. Committing U.S. troops to battle is a high-stakes move, and members of Congress would rather not have to make that decision themselves. It is far easier simply to let the president do it, then give him credit if he called it right and condemn him if he didn't. Moreover, the American people have a history of siding overwhelmingly with presidents who make the call for war; standing in the way is politically risky for any member of Congress—except later, in hindsight, as the current war in Iraq and the earlier war in Vietnam have demonstrated.

None of this was what the Framers envisioned. The Constitution was drafted at a time of deep distrust of monarchy and, indeed, all forms of concentrated power. No single person, our founders believed, should have the responsibility for making the gravest decision a president can make: whether to send young men (and, now, women) into battle. While the world is a very different, more dangerous place than when the country was founded, I find myself in basic agreement with the Founders. In our representative democracy, it is Congress—not the president—that gives voice to the concerns of ordinary Americans.

While it may be too much to expect that, when it comes to the profound issue of war, Congress will suddenly start reasserting itself in a major way, I don't think it's too much to ask it to start rebuilding its competence as a consultative body. Simply put, presidents should consult widely, surely beyond their closest advisers and especially with Congress, before they make the decision to go to war. If the president is determined to send Americans into battle, there is very little anyone can do to stop him. But ensuring that members of Congress and others can ask hard questions before the final decision is made at least offers a chance for wise and cool heads to weigh the risks, and for national policy makers to proceed without blinkers on.

In the end, the calculation is simple. Going to war is the most important decision a government can make, because it means that young people will die. That decision ought not be made by one person, even if that person is the president of the United States.

Initiating Policy

Back during the middle of the George W. Bush administration, there was a small brouhaha when news reports surfaced that a White House official had threatened to fire the chief Medicare actuary if he gave Congress his true estimate of how much the administration's new prescription drug benefit would actually cost.[2] Newspaper editorialists, academics, and commentators all condemned the disregard with which both Congress and the policymaking process were treated in the incident.

One voice was noticeably absent: that of Congress itself. Though a few individual members expressed their concern, I was deeply disappointed that Congress as an institution—perhaps out of party loyalty to the president—failed to express its outrage about being misled by the executive branch.

As Congress considered proposals to reform Medicare, and in particular the drug benefit, it was rightly concerned about the cost of the various alternatives before it. Assured by the administration that its plan would not cost more than $400 billion over the next decade, many members of the House who had previously been undecided decided to support it. So the revelation that the chief actuary had actually estimated the figure to be closer to $534 billion—and that the executive branch had withheld this figure from Congress—was not only embarrassing, it called into question the legitimacy of the policy-making process. Members of both parties should have hit the roof.

Yet there is another even more fundamental issue at stake. Congress and the executive branch are colleagues—equals—in determining the course of the country. Yet even leaving aside the budget and war, Congress over the years has become a hesitant policy maker. The initiative today rests largely with the White House and executive agencies. Small wonder that in this matter of Medicare reform administration officials felt a certain leeway to presume on Capitol Hill's good graces.

There are any number of ways in which the Congress of today exercises just a shadow of the clout it wielded a generation ago, but one of the most important is its reluctance to initiate policy. Congress all too rarely asserts its prerogatives to bring up major issues—such as tax policy or entitlement reform—independently of the president. The United States at the moment faces a crucial series of tests, from rebuilding the economy to reforming health care to protecting our borders, yet Congress often seems to have little to say except in response to administration proposals. Every once in a while it takes the lead in successfully pushing a major issue to the front of the legislative agenda—examples would include the South African sanctions bill in the 1980s or, more recently, the increase in the minimum wage that was approved in 2007—but these have been exceptions.

Why has Congress let slip its responsibilities? Members of Congress themselves give lots of reasons. They range from the legitimate need to tend to their constituents—which now means spending so much time either in the district or en route that only a few days each week can be devoted to national affairs—to the reality that members know one another less well than they used to, especially if they belong to different parties, and are therefore less inclined to work together. And there is also the inclination to defer to the president when he is of the same party. As Robert Kaiser writes,

"Few members put loyalty to the House or Senate ahead of their political loyalty to a Democratic or Republican team."[3]

But that's a political calculation, not necessarily a view of the national interest. Good policy, policy that will stand the test of time, does not evolve when everyone marches to the same drummer. Good policy is the result of hard work, searching analysis, solid information, and respectful argument about what it means. It is the result of people with different points of view, values, and experiences sitting down together to reason with one another and search for common ground. This is precisely what Congress was designed to foster, and it is what we lose when Congress decides that letting someone else take the lead is easier than upholding its rights and duties to initiate policy as the institution that most fully represents the American people.

Understanding Congress

I don't want to suggest that making all of these changes and becoming a vibrant and co-equal branch of government will be easy for Congress. Understanding the institution might help explain why it has been behaving as it does—and why rebuilding it is not as simple as merely deciding that it needs to be done.

For years, I have been describing four core features of Congress to help people better understand the institution and how it works. I think they can also help to explain not only why it is important that Congress become a more forceful branch but also why it will be difficult.

The first thing I say about Congress is that it is a highly *representative* body. This may seem like a cliché, but think for a moment what it means to fulfill the Founders' intention that the people's voices be heard in the halls of government. It means that farmers in Iowa and ranchers in Montana, laborers in Boston, shrimping families in Louisiana, hotel maids in Los Angeles, doctors and lawyers in Minnesota and Georgia—all these and millions of others have someone in Congress who can speak for them. The full diversity of this country's beliefs, concerns, and desires gets funneled to Capitol Hill. This helps to guarantee our freedom, and means that Congress acts with the authority that comes from representing the American people.

Congress is also our most *accessible* branch. You cannot call a Supreme Court justice or the secretary of state to complain about U.S. policy or lodge a grievance. Yet you can call or write your congressional representatives and get a response. And legislators spend much of each week striving to stay in touch with their districts or states: traveling home for long weekends; hosting call-in shows; meeting both in Washington and at home with their constituents. They know what the people they represent are thinking.

You wouldn't want to change either of these characteristics, but when you combine them with a third—the fact that Congress is designed to be a *deliberative* body—you can understand why the institution often seems to drag its feet and have a hard time developing policy. We've got a lot of differences in this country—regional, ethnic, and economic—and issues like taxes, health care, or guns don't lend themselves easily to compromise. People often complain about the pace of the process, but at heart do we want a system where laws are pushed through before consensus is reached? Or one that lacks legislative speed bumps to ensure that multiple views get heard and Americans' rights are safeguarded? This is why Congress often deals with issues incrementally rather than resolving them all at once. Its members have to practice the art of deliberation.

This is especially so because Congress is an extraordinarily *political* body. I mean this to include both the positive and the negative connotations of "political." On the one hand, its members often sway too readily with the currents of public opinion; pay too close attention to the desires of campaign donors; and support or derail legislation for reasons that have little to do with its merits and much to do with seeking partisan or personal advantage. Yet politics as practiced in Congress also entails working hard to understand the concerns of myriad people and interests, bridging differences with an eye toward finding common ground, and building a consensus about how to improve the lives of ordinary Americans.

This is why it's so important that despite all the difficulties Congress fulfill its constitutional mandate as an independent and co-equal branch of government: because it plays a role that the executive doesn't and the courts aren't supposed to. It is the only institution in our federal government charged with listening to the American people, sorting through our needs and interests, and applying both what it hears and its members' own views to the issues of the day. It is an indispensable check on the power of the presidency, and by virtue of its procedures and legislative hurdles, on the power of runaway majorities and the passions of the moment. That is exactly what the Founders envisioned.

3

Strengthening Congressional Oversight

CONGRESSIONAL OVERSIGHT of the executive branch tends to ebb and flow, with periods of strong and useful oversight followed by periods of relative inactivity. Over the past several years, Congress has for the most part ignored its responsibility to keep track of the executive branch, and this has been a serious failure. Tough, continuous congressional oversight holds the president accountable, prevents government missteps, and helps maintain the balance of power between the executive and legislative branches. When it is absent, the federal government and the American people both suffer.

Broken Oversight

A few years back, as charges and countercharges were flying about whether the White House was justified in ordering the invasion of Iraq based on our pre-war intelligence, a simple question was missing. How well, we should have asked ourselves, did the *Congress* do its job during the months leading up to the war?

You could find plenty of critics who argued that the White House and the intelligence community misled the American people about weapons of mass destruction, about Saddam Hussein's ties to Al Qaeda, and about our country's readiness to rebuild Iraq after the war. But there was one group of people who had a special responsibility not to be misled: members of Congress. Congress had access to the same intelligence that the White House was using. Surely, the first exercise of President Bush's doctrine of pre-emptive war deserved some searching exploration and independent judgment before it took place. Instead, it generally met passive acceptance—an attitude that many members of Congress, whichever their party, came to regret. Yet the truth is that the problem went beyond this single instance of rallying around the commander in chief. The deeper, more long-standing problem was that Congress had pretty much forgotten the importance of oversight.

Ordinary Americans aren't the only ones who think of members of Congress primarily as legislators. So do those who spend their days on Capitol Hill. Legislating and tending to constituents, after all, are far more likely to garner attention and votes than delving into the minutiae of executive-branch activity. Yet ever since 1792, when it launched an inquiry into government conduct of the wars against the Indians, Congress has played a crucial role in checking the abuse or misuse of executive powers. It did this in the Teapot Dome scandal of 1923, and more recently in the cases of Watergate and Iran-Contra. During my years in Congress I saw numerous examples of important oversight of the executive branch, such as tough probing of mismanagement at various federal agencies in the early 1980s that led to several resignations and convictions; Representative Henry Waxman's relentless hearings on the need for tougher regulation of the tobacco industry; and investigations into overspending at the Pentagon, including the discovery in 1985 that the Defense Department was purchasing toilet seats for $600 each.

Oversight is often tedious, technical, unglamorous work. Yet at its best it means looking into the nooks and crannies of the government's everyday activities, gauging the impact and success of federal programs, judging whether the expectations that lay behind legislation are being met by executive agencies, and probing for corruption or malfeasance.

Regular oversight throws light on the activities of government. It can protect the country from an imperial presidency, from bureaucratic arrogance, and from the blind pursuit of rules and regulations that, seen in perspective, do more harm than good. It exposes and prevents misconduct, and is one of the few ways of ensuring that the American people have some influence on an administration *after* they vote it into office. Strong congressional oversight, in other words, is essential to the functioning of our democracy. It has always seemed to me that members of Congress owe their allegiance not just to their constituents and their party, but to Congress itself. This means taking seriously their constitutionally mandated role as a branch of government equal in power to the executive that can serve as both a partner and a critic of the White House.

In recent times there's been too little of this. Certainly some good oversight does take place in committees on both the House and the Senate side. But since the 1990s far too much of it has been designed to score political points. As the *National Journal* noted a few years back, the House committee with the most sweeping oversight responsibilities issued no subpoenas to the executive branch during the two years that Congress was under Democratic control and there was a Democrat, Bill Clinton, in the White House. From 1995 to 2000, though, after the GOP took over the House, the committee got busy, handing out well over a thousand subpoenas to Clinton administration officials. Yet most of the effort was devoted to probing Bill and Hillary Clinton's financial affairs rather than to looking carefully at how our government was working.[1] Once the White House changed hands, Congress was happy to look into steroid abuse in professional sports and "diploma mill" universities, but it basically kept its hands off the failure to find weapons of mass destruction in Iraq and the administration's broad definition of its extrajudicial and wiretapping powers. Oversight expanded in the last two years of the Bush administration, when the Democrats again controlled Congress. But even then, some vitally important issues were not carefully explored, most notably lax federal regulation of the housing and finance industries.

To be sure, some basic changes in Congress in recent years have contributed to weakened oversight. As power has become concentrated in the hands of the leadership, for instance, the "authorizing committees"—the committees whose responsibility it is to delve into the activities of specific executive-branch agencies—have met less frequently and exercised far less influence over the budgets of their agencies. Because Congress has been choosing to fund the federal government through the stopgap measures known as "continuing resolutions" or through massive appropriations bills, the routine reauthorization process has largely disappeared; it was during reauthorization hearings that some of the most effective probes of how federal agencies were behaving took place.

There is a cost to all this, and it's not just in lost congressional power. Failing to ask tough questions of the White House and the executive branch allows bureaucrats to become smug and policy makers to sidestep examination of their positions. Not only does the nation benefit from a careful, thorough, and fair congressional probing of the president's policies and assumptions, so does the president.

Every Administration Needs Oversight

Oversight is particularly spotty when the president and the congressional majority share the same party label, for obvious reasons: there's a natural inclination to avoid inquiries that might seem to undermine the president or give ammunition to his political adversaries. Yet it is vital that congressional leaders set that concern aside, for the simple reason that vigorous congressional oversight of the administration—any administration—is necessary for our government to function properly. Under our system of government this is what Congress is supposed to do: to put the national interest first by holding the president and his administration accountable for their actions.

Looking over the shoulder of another party is certainly easier. Yet tough oversight is at least as important when Congress and the administration are of the same party. And it can be done. The $600 toilet seats noted earlier, for example, were brought to the attention of Reagan administration officials by a Republican senator, Bill Cohen of Maine.

Robust oversight need not be viewed as adversarial. Indeed, if presidents understand Congress's constitutional role, they will see its activities as helpful. Constructive oversight brings fresh eyes and insightful questions to the making and implementation of policy. The plain fact is that the executive branch tends to wear blinkers: its officials are there in support of the president, and they are often reluctant to cast critical judgments on his decisions or on the implementation of policy. This last point is particularly important, since Americans have in recent years lost confidence in the federal government not just because of the policies it pursued, but because of its failure to act effectively, whether in Iraq or in helping Louisiana and Mississippi recover from Hurricane Katrina or in overseeing the mortgage and financial-services industries. A Congress that is functioning properly would turn administration officials into regular visitors to Capitol Hill, quiz them relentlessly, and make them explain their policy decisions and how they are implementing federal programs.

For in the end, oversight is not about politics, it's about Congress's responsibility to ensure that the federal government is serving the American people's interests. This is even more important in this day and age, as newspapers shrink their Washington bureaus and, with them, their investigative capabilities.

In 1787, John Adams wrote, "Without three divisions of power, stationed to watch each other, and compare each other's conduct with the laws, it will be impossible that the laws should at all times preserve their authority and govern all men."[2] It is as true today as it was more than 220 years ago.

Oversight Needs to Be Systematic

None of this is to say that, even in the days when it was too lax, Congress failed utterly in its responsibilities. It just took unusual courage from individual members who saw a wrong that Congress might fix and that the American people needed to understand.

Perhaps the best example occurred a few years back, when the Senate Armed Services Committee took up the treatment of Iraqi prisoners at Abu Ghraib. John Warner of Virginia, the committee's chairman at the time, braved the outspoken distaste of his counterparts on the House side and the hesitation of some of his own colleagues, and signaled his determination to pursue his inquiry. "When this situation broke, I felt it was the responsibility of the Congress, a co-equal branch of government, to start hearings," he commented at the time.[3]

There is a world of meaning to be read into Senator Warner's passing reference to Congress as "a co-equal branch of government." It was a small but pointed reminder that the White House, Pentagon, and executive agencies are not the only shapers of official U.S. policies and activities. Congress—the people's branch of government—has not just the right but the duty to be at the table as well. It especially has both the right and the duty to be the body asking those hard questions.

Good congressional oversight is fundamental to our democracy. At its best, it helps Congress—and, through it, the American people—evaluate how well our government and its representatives, whether they're soldiers or bureaucrats, are performing. Congress has of late shown some stirrings of self-respect, and that is a positive development. But to serve the American people and to ensure that we are, indeed, a nation of laws, it cannot rely simply on the determination of a few members at various times to get to the bottom of things. It needs to be assertive as a matter of course.

Congress has several tools for holding federal agencies accountable, including periodic reauthorization, personal visits by members or staff, review by the Government Accountability Office or inspectors general, subpoenas, hearings, investigations, and reports from the executive branch to Congress.

Yet for many years Congress did so little real oversight—as opposed to holding hearings designed to score political points—that it's fair to say its reflexes got rusty. Effective oversight is not just a matter of looking at a few programs; it needs to be part and parcel of Congress's activities, especially in the routine reauthorization process that Congress has by and large abandoned. I once proposed, for example, that each committee do a systematic review of all the significant laws, agencies, and programs under its jurisdiction at least every few years, in part for the substance of what it would find, and in part to keep its oversight abilities fresh.

This is because Congress needs to develop a process for looking continuously over the administration's shoulder, one that impels congressional committees to develop constructive relationships with the agencies they oversee—since excessive antagonism between the branches does little to improve program performance—and to look into the vast range of federal activities that never get into the newspaper headlines.

The point is to make oversight a part of the daily business of Capitol Hill, and to make it as bipartisan as possible. There will certainly be times when the Democratic and Republican leaders of a particular committee disagree, but they should be able to sit down at the beginning of a new Congress and approve the bulk of the committee's oversight agenda. Even more important, for oversight to really work, members must receive a clear message from the congressional leadership of both parties that it is a priority and that it will be done in a bipartisan, systematic, coordinated way.

Most members of Congress see little political benefit in monitoring programs, but for motivation they might pay attention to some of the people who also try to play a watchdog role vis-à-vis the government: newspaper and television news editors. When the war in Iraq was demanding space and coverage, some news executives began to worry about all the activities of the government that were *not* getting covered. "The war is an overriding issue, but that comes with consequences," Tom Rosenstiel, director of the Project for Excellence in Journalism, was quoted as saying at the time. "I'm sure we'll find out in two years that things went unnoticed—things that will come back to haunt us."[4] He was right. Abu Ghraib was one; so were the policies that underpinned the meltdown of the U.S. and world economies in 2007 and 2008.

There is a lesson to be learned from events like Abu Ghraib and the economic meltdown, and it is this: Even in a democracy, things that happen in the shadows can end up having deep implications for the nation and for every American. For the press, it is a professional shortcoming when it fails to bring them to our attention. For Congress, it is a dereliction of its constitutional duties. It is Congress's responsibility to shine light on the workings of government, and to ensure that its actions really do reflect the generous and honorable nature of our country.

4

Restoring the Deliberative Process

WHENEVER I TALK to an audience about congressional process and the importance of maintaining
the regular order in Congress, I can look over the crowd and see
attention start to wander: people shift a little in their seats, their eyes
get a bit unfocused, they look around more at the people nearby. Yet
I continue to include material like this, because these issues matter
deeply to our country. Adhering to its well-established procedures
and restoring the deliberative process would strengthen Congress
considerably as an institution.

Why Congress Needs the Deliberative Process

Not long ago, a group of political scientists asked what
bothered me the most about Congress in recent years. The answer,
I told them, was disturbingly clear: a lack of deliberation.

A few years ago, for example, the House dealt with three significant domestic priorities: tax cuts; a rewrite of Medicare rules to

provide for greater prescription drug coverage; and a bid to create a new energy strategy. Normally, bills on matters of such enormous importance would pass through an extended deliberative process of committee and floor review before going to a final conference committee of the House and Senate—a small group of senior legislators from both houses who work out the differences between the House and Senate versions of the bill. Yet in each case, Congress shortened the normal deliberative process and gave the conference committees the bulk of the responsibility for crafting the legislation, excluding most members of Congress from meaningful involvement. The White House negotiated the final version of the trillion-dollar tax cuts with just three senators and one member of the House. This is not a good way to make laws.

It is no longer unusual when Congress opts for shortcuts, or decides that the majority's goals justify whatever means are necessary to achieve them. Under Republicans and Democrats alike, both houses have been moving in this direction for some time, particularly on important pieces of legislation. It has reached the point where anyone who cares about the integrity of our most representative institution needs to sit up and take notice.

Americans often look with some disdain at the traditional way Congress considers legislation. Why go to all that effort? Bringing an issue before a committee, hearing what witnesses have to say, arguing over amendments to the bill before it even leaves the committee, sending a bill to the floor, arguing again over amendments, debating a final version, and then sending the House and Senate versions off to a conference committee—it can take months, and frequently years, for a particular measure to clear all those hurdles. The process seems convoluted and unwieldy.

But that is because too few Americans understand how much these details matter. The process of deliberation guarantees that their voices are heard and their freedoms protected. Committees are where members of Congress with different backgrounds, political philosophies, and regional outlooks build consensus—in essence, where they make sure that legislation meets the needs of a broad array of Americans.

Committees are also where members and their staff use the expertise they've developed in particular policy arenas to ask hard questions, consider the merits of proposals, and smooth out problems. This is also true of the process once bills leave a committee and move to the floor of the House or Senate. To a large extent, every stage is designed to allow Congress to explore all aspects of a problem, accommodate different interests, reduce points of friction and difference, and build a consensus in support of a bill. This is how Congress knocks out bad ideas and proposals, and adjusts good ideas to make them better laws.

Democracy is first and foremost about process. The Founders understood that *how* we reach a result matters. As congressional scholar Norman Ornstein observed, "The system of checks and balances and the legislative process as it evolved in the House and the Senate were built around deliberation . . . If there is one word at the core of Congress' essence, it is deliberation."[1] The Founders created a system to ensure that all proposals receive careful scrutiny, and that all voices are considered—not just those of a narrow majority.

I realize that as a former member of Congress I risk looking like a fusty old codger tut-tutting the harmless exuberance of a new generation. Certainly, winning policy battles matters for the 535 duly elected senators and representatives, all of whom feel strongly about issues and all of whom want to represent the best interests of their constituents. Yet winning should not be the only thing in a democracy, and what has been happening with increasing frequency in Congress is not harmless. There are real principles at stake these days on Capitol Hill.

When I was in the Congress, I often winced at a comment I heard with growing frequency: "Let's get on with it. We have the votes and we can do whatever we want." If all you care about is winning, perhaps process doesn't matter. But, to my mind, that is not how democracy works.

The democratic process is how we as a society examine the issues confronting us, attempt to reconcile competing views, and try to move forward even when we don't all agree. For this to work, all involved have to feel that, even if the process didn't produce the outcome they wanted, it was still fair—their voices were heard, their opinions considered, all competing options weighed. When those in positions of power within Congress start acting as though these things don't matter, the institution loses legitimacy with its own members, and, more importantly, with the American people.

Omnibus Bills

By now you're probably familiar with one of the worst of Congress's problems: its habit of waiting until the last minute each fall to appropriate money for government agencies, then relying on a massive "omnibus" bill, which is often thousands of pages long and covers thousands of federal programs. Just as predictably, pundits at newspapers around the country then condemn federal lawmakers for hastily putting together a bill that no one can possibly read before it's voted on. Members of Congress ought to listen more carefully to these critics. The simple fact is that by allowing this practice to continue, they're behaving in an undemocratic manner.

In the past, Congress would take up its thirteen individual appropriations bills for defense, agriculture, energy, and so on according to a set schedule, allowing its members to scrutinize the bills with which they were unfamiliar and giving them opportunity to address unpopular or badly written provisions. That well-established process for carrying out Congress's fundamental "power of the purse" has been followed only once since 2001. Instead, many of the separate appropriations bills are combined into huge omnibus bills and brought to the floor of the House and Senate in a form that allows the proponents of the bill to ask a single question: Do we fund the federal government this year or not?

This sounds efficient and practical, so you might wonder what's wrong with it. Let's start with sheer size. Sometimes the bill lands on lawmakers' desks just a day or so—or even less—before they're due to vote on it. The package might contain funding for thousands of federal programs, both large and small. Clearly, it's impossible for legislators to know what they are expected to approve.

Not surprisingly, this offers plenty of opportunity for mischief. A few years ago, for example, a provision was inserted into an omnibus bill that would have allowed members of Congress and their aides unprecedented access to ordinary Americans' tax returns. It was caught only after the bill had been passed by both houses. No member of the House committee responsible for that section of the bill would own up to putting it in, and in the end a committee staffer took responsibility. Our elected representatives, in turn, were faced with the unpalatable choice of saying that they'd known about the measure but chosen to remain silent, or saying that they'd been entirely unaware of—and just approved—a highly controversial piece of legislation written by a nonelected staff member.

Sometimes a much larger issue is involved. One of the factors contributing to the recent financial collapse was that federal banking regulators were prohibited from keeping an eye on the "credit default swaps" which were purchased by many financial institutions to the tune of several trillion dollars. These "swaps" were a major factor in the subprime meltdown and subsequent recession. So why couldn't federal regulators oversee credit default swaps to make sure that there were sufficient funds to back them up? Such oversight was prohibited by a provision added in 2000 to a must-pass omnibus spending bill by a single senator at the very end of the session. A congressional aide later said about the provision, "Nobody in either chamber had any knowledge of what was going on or what was in it."[2]

Over the years, omnibus bills have contained numerous provisions that clearly would not have passed had they come up for a separate vote. It's a process that allows a few legislators—often those in the leadership and members of their staff—to bypass the traditional democratic processes that are supposed to govern Capitol Hill, undermining legislators' accountability to their constituents and the transparency representative democracy needs.

I recognize that there may be times when popular or badly needed legislation is bottled up by a recalcitrant committee chairman or held hostage by delaying tactics, and the only way to bring it to the floor is through some vehicle like an omnibus measure. But it hardly seems worth preserving an omnibus process for such occasions if it is used far more often to evade simple democratic rule.

What is both most frustrating and most encouraging about all this is that nothing terribly dramatic needs to happen to return to a more democratic process. There have been proposals to require that members have at least three days to study legislation before voting on it, and this would be helpful. The real issue, however, is the omnibus practice itself. To fix that, members need to insist that Congress return to the "regular order"—taking up individual appropriations bills on schedule.

There was a time when legislators were keenly aware of the need for such a disciplined habit. On the House floor, when events seemed to be spinning out of control or the leadership appeared to be trying to finagle the process to hide some action it knew could not garner majority support, cries of "Regular order! Regular order!" would ring out. Not long ago, a commentator in the Capitol Hill newspaper *Roll Call* remarked, "Allowing the individual appropriation bills to be considered separately, on their own merits, has become so unusual that it is difficult to even say that it is the 'regular order.'"[3] That is an immensely sad comment on how far ordinary members of Congress have allowed their own prerogatives to be undermined. It should be a call to arms.

Congressional Debates Need Facts, Not Spin

Congress likes to think of itself as "the world's greatest deliberative body," and considering the issues it has to take on, it certainly merits the label. Our senators and representatives face grueling debates on fighting terrorism as a free society, enhancing economic chances for working families, shoring up the financial system, improving the long-term outlook for Social Security, reforming the tax code, and other knotty issues. Congress, after all, is where this diverse nation is supposed to come together to discuss and thoroughly air the challenges we face.

Yet in terms of not just the process, but the *content* of its deliberation, it still has a long way to go. This was brought home most strongly in a 2006 study by two respected political scientists, which stated that thoughtful congressional debate, rooted in facts, is actually hard to come by. Legislators often resort to "half-truths, exaggeration, selective use of facts, and, in a few instances, outright falsehoods," wrote professors Gary Mucciaroni and Paul J. Quirk.[4] This is not reassuring at this especially troubled moment in our history.

We all know that Congress doesn't always live up to the lofty standards we wish it to. Debate on the House and Senate floors can get long-winded, repetitious, and perfunctory. But this study probed deeper than that, exploring how truthful and accurate were claims made during forty-three separate debates between 1995 and 2000 on three key issues of that time: welfare reform, estate-tax reduction, and telecommunications deregulation.

Their conclusion was that in debates, only about a quarter of the claims made by members of Congress were supported by the facts; the other three-fourths were either unsupported or only partially supported by relevant evidence. In addition, "when others exposed speakers' claims as weak, the speakers in almost every case ignored the criticism only to reassert the dubious claims." This brings to mind the infamous comment by Representative Earl Landgrebe of Indiana during the Watergate debate: "My mind is made up," he said. "Don't confuse me with the facts."

Even worse, the authors concluded that "congressional debate is typically no better than moderately informed . . . In a typical debate, the best that Congress achieves is a roughly even balance of fact and fiction."[5]

I suppose this "facts don't matter" approach might sometimes be expected on the campaign trail. There, unfortunately, we have become accustomed to half-truths, distortions, and falsehoods, and voters have had to learn to take campaign statements with a grain of salt. But when Congress is in the process of making decisions on key issues confronting the nation, is it really okay with the American people that its members deal with each other in a straightforward and truthful manner only half the time? I doubt it. Members of Congress simply must do better.

Some internal changes in the way Congress operates would improve the situation, as Mucciaroni and Quirk and others have suggested—extending the time for debate, reducing the number of omnibus bills, and restoring the central role once played by standing committees. Committees usually serve to refine and focus debates on the core issues, making it easier both for the American public and for other members of Congress to follow and take part in them.

In the end, though, I think there's no substitute for members and staff becoming more serious and more careful about how they prepare for and conduct debates. They are, after all, making the nation's laws, not trying to score debating points. The American people have an important role to play in this. They must hold their representatives in Congress to a high standard. They must insist that the decisions of Congress be rooted in solid analysis and factual information. Part of the intense dislike Americans have developed for Congress in recent years stems from disappointment in the quality of its political discourse and the prevalence of spin, distortion, and partisan mockery. As the Congress takes up a long list of formidable public policy challenges, it could go a long way toward restoring public confidence by debating them carefully, fully, and accurately, with respect not only for the truth, but for its own role in making the laws of the nation.

Why Congress Isn't Efficient, and Shouldn't Be

While Congress's shortcomings as a deliberative body may be responsible in part for its low public standing, there is another reason that probably trumps them: the widespread conviction that Congress is simply unable to act to get anything done—on Iraq, on health care, on any of the myriad issues that perplex and trouble the average American.

Wander into any conversation on the topic and you'll get an earful about why this is so: too much partisanship; too much arguing for argument's sake; too many special interests; too much political division in the country. One thing you're unlikely to hear, though, is the mundane but inarguable truth that Congress simply isn't set up to be efficient. It moves by inches for a very good reason: it was designed for deliberation, not speed.

Don't get me wrong. There really *is* too much destructive partisanship on Capitol Hill. There *are* too many people in Congress who confuse their party's talking points with productive debate. Capitol Hill *can* find itself so hemmed in by lobbyists and the expectations of campaign donors that progress becomes impossible. And when the country is up for grabs with divided government and a near-even split in the Congress, making progress is tough. Yet it is also true that by its very nature, Congress is inefficient. And though we might be disappointed sometimes that it can't act faster, in general we're better off as a result.

Think about how Congress was designed by our founders. They wanted to ensure that the body was representative of the American people, and that it provided a forum for reasoned exploration of the issues besetting the nation—in other words, they wanted reflection and deliberation before action. So they created the Senate and the House, which not only provide two different means of representing the country, but require that everything happen twice. Add to that the maze of subcommittees and committees that bills go through and the multiple hurdles they must pass, and it's no surprise that only a small fraction of the bills introduced ever become law. This is an arduous trek for a bill, and it makes for an endless variety of ways in which legislation can be amended or stopped outright. It also, however, provides an opportunity to consider thoroughly the implications and potential effects of each measure.

Beyond its structure, Congress is an immensely complex institution. Power resides not just in the leadership, but also in the committee chairs and ranking minority members, members acknowledged to be experts in a particular field, successful fundraisers, particularly media-savvy members, and others. Then the Senate adds a layer of complexity. There, the ability to filibuster a measure means that effectively it takes sixty votes, not a simple majority, to pass legislation on controversial topics. This is an extremely high bar.

Moreover, Congress's very representativeness is at once its greatest strength and its greatest weakness. This is now such a diverse nation that the assumptions about public policy prevailing in a congressional district in Utah or Mississippi will be very different from, if not diametrically opposed to, those you might find in Los Angeles or much of New England. Congress is where all the varied points of view must grapple with one another, and where all the many private interests at play in the country, those with money and those with nothing but moral suasion, get their say. It's hardly surprising that it can take a while to sort all this out, especially in the House, whose members must stand for election every two years and who therefore are always keenly attuned to the political calendar.

To get a sense of what can happen when Congress does act speedily, look no further than the huge tax cuts approved in 2001 at President Bush's request; he said that taxes could be cut while also reducing the national debt and saving for future initiatives. Instead, annual deficits have soared. Likewise, recall the shock of members when they were later told by the administration that the Medicare prescription bill would cost hundreds of billions of dollars more in its first decade than they'd been led to believe.[6] These bills were rushed through Congress at such a pace that they never got the detailed consideration they needed.

The truth is that Congress deals with the toughest issues in the country. Its job is to understand them thoroughly, weigh the beliefs and interests of an astounding variety of Americans, and consider carefully how to move forward. On the whole, we want to use the brakes on the process provided by the Constitution and by congressional structure; passion and speed are not conducive to good legislation.

Congress Should Not Be Just about Winning

When the House convened in January 2007 and power shifted to the Democrats, those who were watching got treated to a small but revealing moment. As John Boehner, the new minority leader of the House, was handing the House gavel over to the incoming Speaker, Nancy Pelosi, he looked out at the assembled members and told them, "Be nice." It might have sounded like a jocular and insignificant point, but if Congress follows any single admonition, I hope it's that one.

In truth, it shouldn't even need saying. For an individual legislator, cultivating good relationships with other legislators and treating them fairly ought to be a matter of habit. In order to get anything done, you have to work constantly to line up support from fellow members, hear what they have to say, and try to convince them that what you want to accomplish matters. Even if they don't agree with your goals, they'll still respect your efforts.

But treating those in the other party fairly is at the moment as much a group imperative as it is wise personal custom. Congress still hasn't gotten over an extended period in which fair and decent treatment of others was too often downplayed, and it created a toxic environment on Capitol Hill. Those in power have the opportunity to freshen the atmosphere, and every American has a stake in whether or not they make good use of it.

For if there's any single lesson to be gleaned from the Republican takeover after the 1994 elections or the recent shift back to Democratic control, it is that the manner in which a majority wields power has enormous consequences. If members of the minority party lose on issues of policy but believe that the process was a fair one, they might be frustrated but they'll abide by the results. If, on the other hand, they feel constantly slighted, ignored, shut out of the legislative process, and treated overall as if they have nothing to contribute to the national dialogue, they will seethe with resentment. They will do everything in their power to frustrate the majority. And, the vicissitudes of politics being what they are, they will eventually be put back in a position of power.

Which is why I was somewhat disconcerted to see that the Democratic majority in the House, which certainly understands the sting of unfair treatment, has on occasion yielded to the temptation of its newfound power to shut down Republican participation—cutting off minority amendments, using procedural shortcuts, restricting debate. They often seem to forget how damaging mistreatment of the minority can be.

Those in the majority can always come up with reasons for taking shortcuts that allow it to act. That's not the point. The point is that in our democracy, the process is every bit as important as the legislation it produces. Fairness and trust should be the coin of the realm. Congress represents everyone, not just those who voted for members who happen to form the majority. Allowing the regular order of hearings, amendments, and debate to flourish—with fair restrictions to keep it wieldy, if necessary—would go a very long way to healing the scars of the last few years and make it less likely that Capitol Hill will return soon to the ugly bitterness that cost it so much public good will and led to legislative stalemate.

As I said at the beginning of this chapter, internal procedures can seem unbearably arcane and of little import to most Americans. Nothing could be further from the truth. The goal in the House—the most representative institution our nation possesses—is to create a process that is fair and that allows the nation's business to be done, while also letting the minority present an alternative policy, have it debated fully, and then see it voted up or down. The way the majority uses the rules is a basic test of that fairness: if it quashes the minority's ability ever to have its alternatives heard, it flunks.

Now, the House minority bears a share of responsibility, too. If its members are constantly playing little games to score political points, rather than developing serious policy alternatives, then it, too, shares the blame for undercutting the civility and fairness necessary for the House to work. As congressional scholar Norman

Ornstein put it not long ago, "If the minority uses the opportunity to offer amendments to exploit cynically the opening for political purposes . . . it soon will lose its moral high ground for objecting to majority restrictions on debate and amendments."[7]

So far, neither Democrats nor Republicans have covered themselves with glory on this front. The House ought to be a beacon of open, deliberative, and thoroughgoing debate, an institution that truly represents the diversity and fair-minded decency of ordinary Americans. Let us encourage our representatives to make Congress a model of open and fair treatment.

To Govern Well, Return to the Basics

At this moment, with an administration in the White House and newly invigorated majorities in Congress that were all brought into office on promises of "change," there is a fundamental question Washington must answer: If we are to fix our government so that it works competently, effectively, and democratically, how should we go about it? What, in other words, would it take to revive not only our system, but our people's faith in it?

The answer I've been suggesting may seem odd, given how badly askew most Americans believe things had gotten and how desperately they hope for a new order. Rather than "fix" our representative government, I believe that we need to let it function as it was designed to function. We have to return to the basics of our constitutional system, understanding and appreciating its intent and contemplating how this might apply to our vastly changed circumstances today. It's worth remembering that the basic operating manual for our government was written 220 years ago, when we were a much smaller, less complicated, less diverse nation, when communications and events moved much more slowly, and when the sheer breadth and scope of challenges facing the government—while hardly minor—were more manageable. If anything, it's remarkable that our system continues to work even reasonably well.

Returning to the basics means tolerating and encouraging lively debate and thorough deliberation. It means following the well-established regular order which slows things down, gives all sides a chance to be heard, and allows a careful airing of the facts. And it means respecting the voice of those in the minority and making sure that every proposal faces hard questions and tough scrutiny.

We need to accept that there will inevitably be conflict—our system presupposes it—but that winning political battles is not the highest good; rather, resolving conflict within the constraints of the Constitution and according to democratic principles trumps the victory-at-all-costs mentality that has been so prevalent in recent years. Compromise and accommodation, especially in a nation with so many varied interests at play, are the key to policy success and political legitimacy. All of these steps strengthen the Congress as an institution, and help to restore the balance of power with the president that is so essential to the proper functioning of our representative democracy.

Yet even if all these things happen, restoring Americans' faith in the system will require one other thing: patience. While our government needs to respond to the demands of its citizens, under our system the response is typically slow because it's meant to be slow. Our government was not designed to respond to every passing fancy of the people, but rather to give judicious consideration to the nation's needs. Nor can it solve all of our problems. Our representatives may strive to sort out the hopes, desires, and dreams of the American people, and to come up with the best solutions they can, but the plain fact is that some problems are so difficult and our perspectives so varied that no solution might be forthcoming, even when the system is working well.

Our expectations, in other words, need to be high but realistic. We should look for a government that encourages cohesion and political stability, and safeguards individual freedom, prosperity, and peace. If it can do that, then the fact that it can't easily resolve every problem we confront will come to seem a tolerable imperfection, rather than the dismaying infirmity that so many Americans believe it to be today.

5

Reducing Excessive Partisanship

O NE OF THE MOST difficult, deep-seated problems facing Congress is the excessive partisanship that has plagued it in recent years. Yet it is hard to imagine that Congress will ever be able to strengthen itself as an institution without relieving it.

Congress Depends on Civility

When he was just a sixteen-year-old schoolboy, George Washington sat down and copied out 110 "Rules of Civility & Decent Behavior," based on a sixteenth-century set of French maxims. Many of these had to do with simple manners—"Cleanse not your teeth with the tablecloth, napkin, fork or knife," reads Rule 100—but others formed a guide to civil and appropriate behavior in public that our first president followed the rest of his life.

I sometimes wish members of Congress today would adopt the approach taken by that sixteen-year-old. Civil behavior hasn't disappeared from Capitol Hill, but it is far less in evidence than it once was. We are all the poorer as a result.

Why should the behavior of a relative handful of people affect the rest of us so thoroughly? To answer this question, let's start with what I mean by "civility." Simply put, it means that legislators respect the rights and dignity of others. It does not mean that they need to agree with one another—far from it. It is by treating one another civilly that people who *don't* agree still manage to weigh issues carefully and find common ground. We are well served by vigorous debate, but even if our political leaders are not all going to become friends, we can certainly expect them to listen to one another, to respect each other, and to acknowledge that in a nation as divided as we are politically, good governance entails finding solutions that all can live with.

All of this is hard to do these days. Because both houses of Congress were so evenly divided for so long, pretty much everything has come to be seen through a partisan lens, shadowed by the looming presence of the next election. At the same time, some would argue that Congress is also mirroring society as a whole, with its increased harshness and sharper divisions. The media bears some of the blame, since it likes to highlight conflict and political extremes, but in its own way it, too, is reflecting trends around it. Though there are hopeful signs that this may be changing, for a long time strident and even obnoxious behavior has been attracting listeners and viewers and generating respectful attention.

If Congress is merely reflecting the society around it, why should we worry that it has so much trouble making civility its norm? Because on Capitol Hill, the ability of members of Congress to work together directly affects both the quality and the quantity of the work that gets done. Incivility and outright rudeness make it virtually impossible to reconcile opposing views and thus to achieve legislative goals or produce good legislation. In an atmosphere rife with distrust and unpleasantness, it becomes all the more difficult to discuss complex issues, search for reasonable solutions, or build the consensus needed to pass them. If we expect Congress to provide the political leadership this country needs to resolve such difficult problems as the lack of affordable health care or how American workers will pay for retirement, then we must expect its members to work together, regardless of partisan affiliation or ideological differences. In my early years in the House, the Speaker at the time, Carl Albert, drove this point home by telling new members always to remember that each of their colleagues was the duly elected representative of 500,000 Americans, so they owed every one of them the same respect they expected for themselves.

Members of Congress are politicians, and they are sensitive to the dislikes of their constituents. If they believe that they will pay a price for returning home empty-handed or displaying obstinate partisanship, they'll change their behavior. But this means that constituents must make it clear that they do not like divisive name-calling, constantly attacking an opponent's motivation, and blatant partisan calculation. All of us would do well to ponder George Washington's handwritten rules, particularly the first: "Every action done in company, ought to be with some sign of respect to those that are present."

Why Is Congress So Partisan?

Early in my career in the U.S. House of Representatives, I trekked over to the Senate side one day to watch a debate between Hubert Humphrey and Barry Goldwater, two of the great ideological warriors of the era. I don't recall the issue, but I do remember the heat they generated as they went at each other with hammer and tongs—they were knowledgeable, passionate, and deeply committed to their vastly different points of view. I remember just as keenly what happened after they'd fought each other rhetorically: they joked together as they left the floor, heading off to have a drink.

I have a hard time imagining such a scene in today's Washington, where a moment of cross-party camaraderie might be viewed with deep suspicion, as though personal friendship somehow undercuts ideological integrity. In the intensely partisan atmosphere that has reigned on Capitol Hill, it is much less common for two legislators to pursue their divergent beliefs with such intensity of purpose, yet remain fast friends or work together when their interests coincide. This is not to say it doesn't happen; only that it's no longer the rule.

Americans of all stripes have noticed this, too, and they don't like it. The partisanship that divides Congress, along with its members' apparent inability to transcend their divisions, is one important reason the institution's public standing is at historic lows.[1] How did we get here?

In part, the answers lie in a series of long-term political trends that have converged to create this current unhappy mood. Computers, for instance, have enabled state legislators—or members of Congress eager to dictate to them—to draw with great precision congressional district lines that create safely Democratic or Republican districts. The result is that most politicians running for the U.S. House don't have to appeal to the political center to win, they just need to appeal to the core of their parties' supporters.

There has also been a marked shift over the past generation in how we view the government. When I first entered national politics in the 1960s, the prevailing attitude toward the federal government was that it had its place in life, but that place was fairly limited. "Keep the government off my back" was the sentiment I heard most frequently. Over time, though, people began turning to Washington for help: a subsidy here, a tax break there, a program or a grant targeted to their needs. By the 1990s, they were streaming into the city to state their case. Since the end of 2008, of course, the federal government has come to be seen as an indispensable actor in rescuing the private economy. All of this is a huge attitudinal shift, and it has intensified our politics and raised the stakes in Congress.

For their part, many politicians and party leaders have over the last decade or so moved away from the old values of compromise, accommodation, and civility to reap whatever advantage they could from political division. This started at the very top. Presidents have typically believed in using their office to expand their political base; President George W. Bush, on the other hand, governed so as to appeal to his existing base, and that approach was largely echoed on both sides of the aisle in Congress. Legislative tactics leaned far more toward excluding the minority than toward seeking ways to work with all members. That made Congress an increasingly angry place, as the minority chafed under its restrictions and the majority still saw red over slights it suffered when it was in the minority.

Parties have also been pushed to their ideological extremes by the interest groups that fund and try to influence them. Outside Washington, the constituencies that make up "we, the people" have become ever more sharply etched. Ethnic minorities are more of a presence in politics than they were a generation ago, as they scramble to move up the economic ladder and speak with a louder voice in the political arena. Special-interest voters—environmentalists, gun-rights backers, abortion-rights advocates, religious conservatives—have become more firmly self-identified and catered to by politicians. As members become spokesmen for particular points of view, their positions take on a harder edge, since they are playing to potential campaign funders or to an interest group whose supporters' votes they need at election time.

The electorate, too, is politically divided, which often manifests itself in a Congress that is narrowly controlled by one party and faces a president of the other. In recent decades, each party has been struggling to become the majority party, and so every vote on Capitol Hill has taken on heavily partisan implications, since the leadership hopes that by taking the position it does—and forcefully encouraging rank-and-file members to go along—it will pick up a few extra seats at the next election. This invites partisan struggle.

These political trends have been reinforced by changes within Congress. If it is hard to find moderates there, it is even harder to find *institutionalists*, people who worry about the role of Congress as a separate and independent branch of government and who focus on strengthening Congress as an institution. Giving pride of place to partisanship and political calculation erodes Congress's role as a deliberative body; "debate" these days is often two sets of talking points hammering at each other, rather than a genuine effort to reach consensus on the best course for the American people to follow. Members worry less about how Congress might carry out its constitutional responsibilities and more about what gives their party an edge.

Even something as mundane as the congressional schedule now encourages partisanship. As their time on Capitol Hill has come to focus on committee hearings, floor debate, and other opportunities for confrontation, and as their weekends now are often taken up with travel back to their states to meet with constituents, members of Congress in recent years have found far fewer opportunities to develop the kinds of friendships that cross party lines—and that produced such close friendships as Humphrey and Goldwater's. Too often, members today see those across the aisle not as colleagues but as adversaries.

These are all deep-seated trends, and they will not be easy to reverse, despite the respite from intense partisanship that took hold just after the 2008 presidential election. Yet I take great hope from the fact that the bulk of the electorate simply wants to see the challenges that confront them—and us, as a nation—addressed pragmatically. They want commonsense approaches, not ideologically driven ones. They want to see politicians striving to find common ground, not dwelling on their differences, and working for the common good, not promoting special interests. Eventually, if it's repeated often enough and firmly enough, that message will stick with our political leaders.

Why Holding the Majority Matters

When you see news stories about which party is likely to emerge from the next election with a majority in Congress, keep one thing in mind: the basement. You might think that congressional leaders care most about the ability that majority status gives them to advance their legislative agenda, and you'd no doubt be correct; but rest assured that they're also thinking about the gloomy corridors underneath the various House office buildings on Capitol Hill.

This is where members of the minority party in the House often get relegated when they host a gathering for constituents or visitors, while members of the majority are meeting in rooms that showcase the grandeur of Congress—the elegant ones just off the

House floor in the Capitol, with high ceilings, plush carpets, and rich wood paneling.

I tell you this because it helps to illustrate why members of Congress behave as they do when control of their chamber is at stake. Being in the minority means major changes like losing the House or Senate leadership, committee chairmanships, and the opportunity to set and advance a party's agenda. But that's just the start of it. The difference between being the majority party and the minority party is so great that in many ways their respective members have two very different experiences of Congress. This is one reason the intense partisanship we've seen on Capitol Hill for well over a decade now has such a sharp edge to it.

Party status affects pretty much everything. The majority not only gets nicer spaces and meeting rooms, it also gets to determine which members and staff will go on overseas fact-finding trips, and much more. Members of the majority party enjoy all sorts of little perks that make life on Capitol Hill more pleasant. On congressional committees, the majority might take three-fourths of the budget and have three times the number of staff as the minority, so a shift in party control can be traumatic for those who find themselves suddenly in the minority.

Then, of course, there are the policy-making differences. In the House, for instance, the leadership of the majority party completely controls the legislative agenda. It decides not only which issues will be taken up, but how they can be debated, whether amendments will be allowed, and how the matter will be handled on the House floor. If it wished, it could—and on occasion does—prevent the minority party from offering any amendments at all to important bills brought up on the floor. The rules are somewhat less lopsided in the Senate, though even there it is easier for senators in the minority to obstruct legislation than it is to help shape it.

The result of all this is that in a closely divided Congress, the stakes in each election are enormous, in terms not only of which policies and philosophies will prevail, but of what legislative life will be like for members of each party; this in turn fosters an atmosphere of partisanship and mistrust, and makes it harder to cooperate across the aisle, because neither party wants to give the other the slightest advantage. Americans may be tired of the partisanship they've seen on Capitol Hill, but it's worth knowing that there are some basic institutional forces at work that make it difficult to overcome.

None of this is to say that lessening partisanship is impossible— just that it won't happen unless the majority and the minority in both houses of Congress make a concerted effort to behave in ways that narrow the vast gulf in potential power and perquisites. How the majority treats the minority, and vice versa, is hugely important in terms of setting the atmosphere and tone on Capitol Hill.

For the majority's part, this means being aware that it sets the tone, and that consulting with members of the minority party— treating them fairly, as colleagues and not as enemies—should be a normal part of doing business. Equally important, the minority has a responsibility not to gum up the works by taking advantage of arcane rules of procedure or trying to turn every iota of legislative business to its political advantage. The tone overall ought to be one of mutual respect and fairness, ruled by a constant awareness that Congress is there to serve the American people and to make the country work, not to offer the two parties an arena in which to duke it out for political advantage. Only then can the people who serve in Congress free themselves from the institutional forces that of late have made it such an unpleasant place for many of them to serve.

How Do We Reduce Partisanship?

I don't want to give the impression here that I'm starry-eyed about politics. It's a contact sport, and hard-hitting partisan competition is unavoidable, even desirable. It offers clear choices and different approaches to solving our problems, and it enhances the accountability of those in power when the other side is willing to point out weaknesses in their thinking or their performance.

Still, the country at large yearns for less polarization these days, and believes that partisan engagement has gone too far. Even

Washington insiders acknowledge that the extreme partisanship of recent years has made it more difficult to govern productively, leading more often to stalemate than to policy advances. They go to great oratorical lengths to deplore how partisan Congress has become. Acknowledging the problem, though, is easier than knowing what to do about it.

So what can we do? The first step must be taken by American voters. However slowly, Congress responds to what its members hear back home. A drumbeat of dislike for mean-spirited partisanship and insistence on working through differences will eventually get through. Members of Congress must be held responsible for the kind of institution they inhabit.

It was a very positive sign in the 2008 presidential campaign that when a candidate would go too far with negative, personal attacks, the voters made it clear that they just didn't want to see that, and the contest would become somewhat more civil. So the voice of the people does get through.

There's a tougher nut to crack, too: it has to do with rebuilding the strength of the dormant center in American politics. On this front, there are any number of steps that might make little difference alone, but together could add up to a sea change in how Washington operates.

One of them is already happening: the rise of the internet for fundraising. The ability to go over the heads of well-heeled special interests and fund a campaign through the small donations of ordinary Americans has the potential to rewrite political candidates' loyalties once they're in office. The less financial influence wielded by groups with a specific cause, the better the chance that our essential moderation as a nation will be reflected in Washington.

Equally important is a growing restlessness with how congressional districts get drawn. For the most part, district maps are designed by state legislatures, which often defer to the wishes of their congressional delegations. Somehow, these maps always produce safe districts for one party or the other, instead of competitive districts that would produce candidates adept at forging coalitions of independents and moderates of both parties. Turning redistricting over to independent commissions charged with crafting districts based on commonality of interest and geographic compactness, rather than partisan affiliation, would make a significant difference.

There is work to be done on Capitol Hill, too, though it might not seem like work: legislators need to get to know one another. It is hard to attack someone you know well. Yet the congressional schedule—constant travel back home to meet with constituents, the need to raise money, the pressures of campaigning—keeps members of Congress and their families out of Washington, away from their colleagues, and far less likely to find time for forging friendships across partisan lines.

The congressional leadership bears a special responsibility for setting the overall tone of the institution. Party leaders on both sides of the aisle need to step up and make it clear to their members that a civil working environment is a top priority. A clear message from the top is one of the most important steps that could be taken to rein in the excessive partisanship plaguing the Congress.

It's also particularly important for members of Congress to look deliberately for issues that hold the hope of successful bipartisanship. Our nation's need for investment in its aging infrastructure—its roads, bridges, and transportation networks—offers one such possibility. It's not a partisan issue; it's a good governance issue.

Then, once Democrats and Republicans on Capitol Hill have come together to resolve a few problems like this, they may come to understand what ordinary Americans have known for some time: that the only way to solve our really tough problems—health care, energy independence, the rise of terrorism, the challenges posed by globalization—is to work together as a nation. In a nation as politically diverse as ours, leaders who know how to emphasize the common purpose—rather than their own party's monopoly on the truth—will ultimately be the ones to lead us from our current partisan morass.

6

Strengthening Ethics Enforcement

MANY MEMBERS of Congress would see no reason to include a chapter on ethics reform in a book on strengthening Congress. They see no connection between a vigorous ethics process and a stronger, more effective Congress. Well, they might not, but their constituents do.

Congress Needs to Invigorate Its Ethics System, Not Weaken It

It's not often that standing still can make headlines, but Congress managed to do just that a few years ago, when the House leadership decided to abandon two rules changes it had proposed. One would have made it more difficult for legislators to discipline a colleague for ethics violations. The other would have allowed the House majority leader to keep his position even if he was indicted by a grand jury back home.

House members are due a small measure of applause for stopping these moves, but true congratulations should go to ordinary

American citizens. The Republican majority of the time decided to drop the two proposals after many of its members pressured their leaders to backtrack. Why did they do this? Having spent time during the end-of-the-year recess listening to complaints from constituents, they understood that weakening ethics provisions would reflect poorly on themselves, their party, and the House itself. The common sense of American voters, who were willing to speak up to their elected representatives, won the day.

Take the former Republican leadership's proposal to abolish the thirty-year-old rule allowing members of the House to be rebuked for bringing discredit on the institution even if they did not violate the law. Instead, the leadership wanted House members to get a pass unless they violated a specific law or rule. This idea actually had a fair amount of support among incumbent members of Congress. But is it really too much to expect that the people we entrust with safeguarding our democracy will conduct themselves at all times to reflect creditably on the House? Obviously, Americans didn't think this is unreasonable—that's why they let their representatives know what they thought about the rules changes.

But isn't it enough that if members of Congress break the law, they can be prosecuted? In a word, no. Ethical misbehavior comes in so many shapes and sizes that if you have to spell out every possible violation, a member bent on mischief can always find ways to skirt the rules. Once we get away from broad standards of good conduct, we fall into legalese and loopholes. And I don't think we want to defer to prosecutors and the courts when it comes to judging our elected representatives. "At least he's not a convicted felon" does not strike me as the standard this nation ought to set for its lawmakers. We can do better.

There's also a more fundamental issue at stake. James Wilson of Pennsylvania, a member of the Constitutional Convention who was rivaled only by James Madison in his grasp of the principles at issue in forging a democracy, argued that the behavior of the government depends on the character of those entrusted to guide it. "As the conduct of a state, both with regard to itself and others, must greatly depend upon the character, the talents, and the principles of those to whom the direction of that conduct is intrusted," he said, "it is highly necessary that those who are to protect the rights, and to perform the duties of the commonwealth, should be men of proper principles, talents, and characters." At the same time, he pointed out, the ultimate responsibility lies with the voters, who need to be able to "distinguish and select" those with the proper integrity.[1]

Voters want their elected representatives to be men and women of integrity. But they don't always know about their representative's misbehavior, and sometimes they fail to vote the scoundrel out of office. That's where Congress comes in. Congress should set high standards for itself and then enforce them. Only then will it measure up to the expectations of the voters, and reclaim their respect and confidence. It should listen to ethics complaints, investigate them fully and fairly, and punish transgressions without a lot of hemming and hawing. That's what Americans want, and they deserve to have it.

Why Ethics Should Matter to Congress

Why do Americans get so upset with the ethical misdeeds of members of Congress? Certainly one of the surest ways for members to be defeated at the polls—no matter how many crazy votes they may have cast over the years—is to be caught accepting lavish, unreported gifts from lobbyists, having improper sexual contact with congressional pages, or enriching themselves by pushing for a new road or bridge in their district that just happens to increase the value of their property.

Maybe it's because these are matters that every voter can understand, compared to the intricacies of the budget process, foreign policy, or financial institution reform. But I think it goes much deeper than that. Part of the answer is suggested by the research of two University of Nebraska political scientists, John Hibbing and Elizabeth Theiss-Morse.[2]

Most political scientists thought that the voters cared about policy and very little about process—the final bill that emerged and not the complicated legislative process that produced it. But extensive polling and interviews convinced Hibbing and Theiss-Morse otherwise, they wrote in their 1995 and 2002 books about public attitudes toward Congress: Americans care a great deal about the process, and are often upset about it. In surveying opinion about the 1991 confirmation of Clarence Thomas as a justice of the U.S. Supreme Court, they found that people were bothered less by his confirmation than by the process that led up to it: the makeup of the committee, the way members questioned the witnesses, the tone of the proceedings, the way allegations were handled.

Americans also tend to be troubled by some of the most fundamental behaviors in Congress—the disagreements, bickering, and compromises. One of their most basic concerns about the process, Hibbing and Theiss-Morse found, was that it be "non-self-interested": they want the legislative process to be fair and not biased in favor of lobbyists bearing gifts or members of Congress looking out for themselves.

In other words, maintaining high standards of ethical conduct is not peripheral to the proper functioning of Congress, it lies at the heart of it. It is essential to its legitimacy.

I have always thought that the vast majority of members of Congress are honest, hardworking legislators, and I expect that most of the legislators on Capitol Hill today feel similarly. Close as they are to daily legislative life, they may not always see the need for vigorous ethics enforcement—especially if they expect their political opponents to use it against them or other members of their party.

That is too narrow a consideration, though. It ignores the interests of the institution itself, and undermines the foundation on which public trust in democratic institutions is built. Maintaining high standards of congressional conduct in a robust, credible, transparent way helps to reestablish basic trust in an institution that touches on the lives of every American. If we have confidence in the judgment and integrity of our leaders, our representative democracy is strengthened.

Getting Outside Help

This being the case, it seems inescapable that Congress will only regain the faith of ordinary Americans when members of Congress are viewed as people of integrity. Yet that still appears to be a long way off.

I see no other way to read the results of a recent poll by the Center on Congress at Indiana University. When it asked 1,000 people whether "most members of Congress are honest people of good character," a rather stunning 42 percent said they are not. Asked to grade Congress on holding its members to high ethical standards, 75 percent gave it either a D or an F.[3]

This dismal view of members' integrity—and of their interest in upholding the institution's integrity—is especially striking given the importance the general public places on it. Asked which characteristic they consider to be most critical in a member of Congress, respondents to the poll rated honesty as by far the most important, surpassing a member's positions on issues, religious convictions, good judgment, or ability to get things done.

Given the weight the public places on honesty, you'd think that members of Congress would be falling all over themselves to demonstrate that they can put their houses in order. Yet the ethics committees of both the House and the Senate have been far too supine in recent years, even as an array of scandals hit their institutions.

Over a dozen members of Congress have come under federal investigation for everything from improper ties with lobbyists to bribery to using their influence for personal benefit. One is now in federal prison for accepting a staggering $2.4 million in bribes. Recently, some members have been accused of steering earmarks to campaign contributors, others of getting special deals for themselves or their families in housing or other ways. Few academics or journalists would say that congressional ethics enforcement has worked, a sentiment shared by the general public.

The signals in 2006 from the new incoming House Speaker, Nancy Pelosi, were quite positive. She said that the 110th Congress would be "the most honest, most open and most ethical Congress in history,"[4] and the new House majority quickly began to put together a package of reforms. Republican leaders also supported efforts to prevent abuses of office.

The result was that a meaningful package of ethics reforms passed the House quickly. By overwhelming majorities, members voted to ban the acceptance of gifts from lobbyists, including meals and tickets to sporting events, and also severely restricted lobbyist-paid trips—no more of those now-infamous golfing trips to Scotland. They also prohibited staff members from accepting travel on corporate jets and toughened the disclosure requirements on earmarks. A similar ethics package passed the Senate. The free-wheeling atmosphere that once prevailed on Capitol Hill—at least until the Jack Abramoff scandal dampened the fun—was to become a thing of the past.

Yet despite these needed reforms, ethics committee action against members of Congress charged with misconduct has generally remained lax. Enforcing ethics standards sounds like it should be fairly straightforward, but there are some deep-seated factors working against it.

Having served on the ethics committee when I was in the House, I know how difficult an assignment it can be. Passing judgment on one's friends and colleagues is hard, there's no question about that. Not only do members of Congress need one another in order to be effective, they feel an entirely natural reluctance to judge the ethics of their peers in public. The slap-on-the-wrist approach taken by the House ethics committee toward members who knew early on about former representative Mark Foley's behavior toward House pages is a classic illustration of how hard it is for Congress to enforce its own ethics code.

This is a big reason for a promising step taken by the House: the establishment of an outside review board to investigate ethics complaints. This Office of Congressional Ethics, made up of an equal number of Democrats and Republicans who are not sitting House members, has the authority to look into complaints about misconduct, dismiss frivolous or politically motivated accusations, and make recommendations to the full ethics committee for further investigation and sanctions. As political scientist Thomas Mann—a longtime proponent of ethics reform—points out, legislators in various states and in other countries have set up independent ethics entities and found they work well. It is time for substantive change in Congress, as well.[5]

As with many things on Capitol Hill, the proof will be in the implementation. The new review board does not have subpoena power, and at least one of its Democratic members and one of its Republicans have to agree that an investigation has merit before it can move forward—a recipe that could lead to partisan stalemate. Moreover, once an investigation starts, the board needs to have credible power to conduct its inquiries, and the political and financial resources to give it heft.

The fact that Congress has to look for help from an outside panel is disappointing; it indicates that it is unable to police its own members. But it is also a recognition of the political reality that the congressional ethics process has in recent decades become highly politicized. Too often, complaints of impropriety were made not to strengthen the institution or uphold its integrity, but to weaken a political opponent and drive a member from office with ethics attacks when substantive attacks on his or her record didn't work. When I was in the House, some of the "ethics and corruption" charges made against the leaders of both parties were accurate, some were greatly exaggerated, and some were simply false. Among other things, the charges led to the resignation of Democratic Speaker Jim Wright, to a steep fine against Republican Speaker Newt Gingrich, and to a bitter, poisonous atmosphere on Capitol Hill. The politicization of the ethics process was getting out of control.

One of the core goals of this outside panel is to reduce the political misuse of the ethics process, and that is certainly needed. Not punishing ethical misconduct has weakened the institution, but so has the politically motivated misuse of the process by members of both parties. Both bring discredit on the institution and both contribute to the low opinion people have of members' integrity.

So I see the creation of an independent Office of Congressional Ethics as a positive step forward. The reform is trying to address basic problems that have long plagued House ethics enforcement: on one hand a hesitancy to investigate friends and colleagues, and on the other a willingness to go after political opponents for purely political reasons. Even though an independent panel can at best make recommendations for enforcement to the ethics committee, its words will carry great weight and ensure that, at a minimum, the American public will have a trustworthy yardstick by which to judge the actions—or inaction—of its representatives.

It takes two forces acting at once to keep congressional ethics on the front burner. One is pressure from the voters. Large numbers must say that corruption and scandals in government are extremely important to how they vote; public pressure is a key influence at the moment. The other is a clear message from the bipartisan leadership of the House and Senate that this is important, and that they expect and will enforce the highest standards of conduct in Congress. Strict and timely enforcement cuts both ways—it punishes members who have stepped over the line, but also clears the names of members who have been unjustly accused.

There will no doubt be attempts ahead to weaken the various reforms that have been adopted, just as the temptation once the spotlight has moved on will be to let standards slip. But as long as the public and the congressional leadership remain determined to see that members of Congress act to reflect credit on the institution and to live up to what the American people expect and deserve, we have a good chance of regaining a strengthened institution that makes us proud and maintains our trust.

7

Curbing the Influence of Lobbyists

THE POWER OF LOBBYISTS in our system of government troubles Americans deeply and often makes
them question the basic integrity of the legislative process. They
wonder whether a given bill passed because it's best for the country, or because those with money had extraordinary opportunities
to influence legislators that ordinary citizens lacked. They even
wonder whether their representatives actually heard the voice of
the people. In a recent Center on Congress survey, citizens were
asked who members of Congress listened to most. Their answer?
Lobbyists (51%), then party leaders (38%), then the voters back
home (11%).[1] When ordinary Americans come to believe that our
democratic system of government does not work for them, that's a
serious problem.

We Pay a Price for Special-Interest Lobbying

President William McKinley isn't remembered for much
these days, other than perhaps calling for war with Spain after the

sinking of the *Maine,* and being assassinated in 1901. But you might give him a moment's thought for one other thing: his insistence that he didn't want any lobbyists serving in his administration.

In recent years we have become accustomed to the presence of lobbyists in every nook and cranny of Washington. People serve in one president's administration, leave it to make more money lobbying, then return to serve someone else in the White House. They run major D.C. lobbying firms, then show up as key advisers to the presidential candidates. They put in time on Capitol Hill, either as staffers or as members of Congress, then turn around to lobby their former colleagues. And if they don't become lobbyists themselves, they marry them. Any number of sitting members of Congress go home to dinner with spouses who work for private lobbying firms or represent particular special interests on Capitol Hill.

It makes sense for talented people to pursue positions of power and influence. Yet we do pay a price for the special-interest lobbying that has become so common in Washington: loss of public confidence in the system. Our system is built on the notion that citizens should have access to their representatives—and we do. But many Americans perceive a real difference between their letters, e-mails, and attendance at the occasional public meeting and the attention that the lobbying corps commands.

Let's start with the basics. Lobbying is a huge business. There are roughly 35,000 registered lobbyists, but that does not include the marketers, consultants, public relations experts, pollsters, support personnel, and others who back up their work. One expert on lobbying, American University government professor James Thurber, puts the total number of people involved in lobbying at more than 250,000.[2] This army of people—whose activities, remember, are aimed at influencing just 535 members of Congress and a relative handful of federal officials—cost and spend several billion dollars each year. The drug industry alone, for example, has spent $1 billion in lobbying Capitol Hill over the last decade.

What do we as a nation get for this unbalanced "access"? On the one hand, lobbying unquestionably has a role to play in the

conversation on Capitol Hill about policy. Lobbyists' most fundamental currency is information, and the more it can be trusted, the
more successful the lobbyist will be; that is why, over the years, the
quality of the lobbying corps has grown. Lobbyists represent many
different slices of our nation—you are almost certainly represented
in Washington by *someone,* whether it's the AARP or the Sierra
Club or the National Rifle Association—and, as a result, they make
it possible for many citizens to participate indirectly in the policy-
making process. Perhaps most important, lobbyists educate both
members of Congress and the general public about key issues facing
the country—and because there are so many of them, it's unlikely
that any single interest will dominate all the others.

At the same time, the process sometimes leads to legislation or
regulations that are clearly tilted in favor of those willing to invest
a lot of money in order to reap even greater returns. We see this in
our extraordinarily complex tax code, which goes out of its way to
favor particular interests, and which often costs the U.S. Treasury—
you and me, in other words—billions of dollars in forgone revenue.
We also see it in federal spending bills that give huge subsidies for
well-connected businesses; special earmarks that may have a representative's name on them but were often submitted on behalf of
a lobbyist and his or her clients; and regulations or interpretations
of federal law that favor those well-organized and rich enough to
prevail over what most people would consider the national interest.
There are lobbyists who brag that the money their clients spend on
lobbying materially rewards those clients, paying a high return on
their investment when their policy preferences are made into law.

In some ways, the problem isn't lobbying per se, but the lack of
transparency that surrounds it. In a representative democracy we
depend on the accountability of our legislators and on knowing how
they arrive at the decisions they do; yet weak reporting requirements
undermine our ability to know about all of the lobbying aimed at
affecting the votes of our representatives. Our system's legitimacy
rests on lawmakers' owing their attention and their allegiance to
the ordinary people who sent them to Washington; yet too many

Americans now believe—because they don't see evidence to the contrary—that the voters have been surpassed by big campaign contributors, corporations that provide fancy dinners at plush resorts or put their private jets at legislators' disposal, and the lobbyists who organize these inducements. We want to believe that we, the people, can be heard in the halls of power, and that the interests of every side will be fairly weighed as legislation and regulations are crafted; yet many Americans are now convinced they don't stand a chance against wealthy special interests.

Special interests' impact on Washington is hardly all bad. Over the years, I have seen many "special interests" representing a broad cross-section of Americans contribute to our nation's advancement: leaders in business, labor, education, environment, religion, and civil rights. Many of them have made outstanding contributions to the common good. But in recent years, money and a willingness to spend it to promote narrow and particular interests have become defining components of "clout" in Washington, and this has bred a level of cynicism about the system that is unmatched in my four decades of involvement in politics. That is unquestionably the most pernicious effect that special-interest lobbying has had on our system. We cannot sustain indefinitely this erosion of public confidence in our system.

Lobbying Murkiness Undermines Our Trust in Congress

Indeed, I would argue that it is not the occasional scandal that is most threatening to Congress's stability. True, stories of influence-peddling schemes or members of Congress going to prison for bribery certainly make the headlines, but I wish lobbying came in for more than just sporadic scrutiny. The disturbing fact about Congress is how little we actually know about the influence wielded by lobbyists—and the people who pay them—on the everyday workings of government.

The thousands of registered lobbyists who are paid to shape federal decision making are a fact of life in Washington, as any member of Congress who meets them every day in his or her office, in the hallways, even in the restroom, can tell you. When an important vote is pending, you cannot walk from your office to the floor of the House or Senate without bumping into hordes of them, lined up to signal with a thumb up or down how they're hoping you will vote. It can be annoying, but there's nothing harmful about that.

What *is* harmful is how shrouded in secrecy the lobbying game often turns out to be. In most cases, what lobbyists do is sit down and try to make the strongest case they can for a given cause—sharing information and adding perspectives a member of Congress might not have thought about. If that were all that was involved in a lobbying campaign, there wouldn't be much to worry about. Unfortunately, a lot of money has been spent on wining and dining members of Congress, treating them to rounds of golf, flying them to warm or exotic locales, and underwriting their campaigns. There may be no direct connection between a member's vote and that sort of treatment, but the well-heeled don't spend their money idly.

It's possible that there is no way consistent with First Amendment protections of free speech to level the playing field for those without resources. Still, there is an antidote: public information and opinion. Many private interests would rather the public not know that their money lies behind this or that cause on Capitol Hill. These are the people, companies, and groups that form organizations and trade associations with innocuous names like "the Association for Freedom," which then go about their business of promoting special-interest legislation with no one the wiser. Our challenge as a society is to create and pass lobby disclosure laws with teeth, so that no matter how someone spends money to influence legislation, the rest of us will know it.

The laws have been far too docile in this regard. While the 1995 Lobbying Disclosure Act was supposed to make the activity more transparent, the Center for Public Integrity recently reported that "the federal disclosure system is in disarray." Roughly one in five of the companies registered to lobby failed to file required forms, and overall, 14,000 documents that should have been filed were missing, while another fifth of the required lobbying forms were filed late.

The center also found that "countless forms are filed with portions that are blank or improperly filled out. An unknown number of lobbyists neglect or refuse to file any disclosure forms whatsoever."[3] In essence, we have had a lobby disclosure system in name only. Rigorous disclosure cuts both ways: it exposes the improper acts of some, but it also lets the public know that many lobbyists perform their work carefully and honestly. If we are to restore faith in Congress without limiting the free-speech rights of lobbyists, I believe the only way is to bring lobbying as much as possible into the light of day, so that ordinary Americans can understand how their representatives arrived at the decisions they did and then decide whether or not they feel comfortable with how the process worked.

There is much that could be made public that has either been hidden or rendered so inaccessible that it might as well be. Campaign donations and lobbying expenses, for instance, should promptly be published online and made easily searchable, so that we know right away who is financing whom and to what end. New technology makes possible a degree of scrutiny that would have been inconceivable even fifteen years ago. Without making a special trip to Washington or scouring some obscure federal office for a buried report, we could know immediately which special interests fund the campaigns of specific members or devote millions of dollars to buying access (if not more) to members of Congress. We could know right away when a member attaches an innocuous-seeming amendment to a bill that happens to benefit a major campaign contributor. Congress recently took several positive steps along these lines to give the public more information about the work of lobbyists. It needs to make sure that these reforms are strictly enforced, and it needs to continue its reform efforts. Democracy, after all, is a process, not a result; Americans need to see that process.

This is not just a matter of fairness. It goes to the heart of congressional legitimacy. Supreme Court Justice David Souter once said, "I think most people assume—I do, certainly—that someone making an extraordinarily large contribution is going to get some kind of an extraordinary return for it. I think that is a pervasive assumption."[4] It is also a harmful one, undermining the faith of ordinary Americans in our political system. We might not be able to limit these contributions, but we should certainly know who made them and to whom, and hold our elected representatives to account for their behavior as a result.

True Lobbying Reform

After many months of watching its public image take a shellacking as a result of the Jack Abramoff lobbying scandal, Congress finally started to move on lobby reform. With all the enthusiasm of a convert to the cause, it has been awash in ideas for curtailing the practices that have so embarrassed the Capitol.

Pretty much every aspect of lobbyists' relations with Capitol Hill has been up for debate. After taking over control of the House in 2007, the Democrats, with Republican support, passed a series of measures that banned gifts from lobbyists, tightened restrictions on lobbyist-paid travel for members and staff, and banned travel on corporate jets. There are proposals to lengthen the period between the time a member of Congress or high-ranking staffer leaves Capitol Hill and when he or she can start lobbying. And there are demands that Congress create an Office of Public Integrity with the ability to investigate possible breaches of lobby laws and the power to refer what it finds to congressional ethics committees and the Department of Justice.

These are worthwhile ideas. Yet even if we enact them all, we will have at best skirted the real issue.

Don't get me wrong. You have to start somewhere. Banning trips by members of Congress that are paid for by private interests, for instance, makes plain common sense. If a trip is in the public interest, then the government should pay for it. If it's not, then why risk the appearance of a too-cozy relationship with some special interest? Similarly, full disclosure of all lobbying activities is a simple necessity. And if we're going to have such laws on the books, then creating some sort of enforcement body with sharp teeth is vital.

We have plenty of lobbying laws already, but they are so rarely enforced that lobbyists consider them a joke. If we're going to have rules, let's enforce them.

Still, the heart of the matter is not travel or gifts or even enforcement. The issue that underlies all else is money. Simply put, politicians who want to be reelected today are desperate for money, because elections are extraordinarily expensive. On the other side, lobbyists just as desperately want to influence legislation. And the tool they have at their disposal is the substance that politicians crave.

Lobbyists have endless ways of pumping money into the system. It's not just the billions of dollars they spend each year to influence the federal government. It's also their expanding role in filling a candidate's campaign coffers. They fund campaign events. They solicit and bundle large campaign contributions from their clients. They underwrite "independent" campaigns targeting members' campaign opponents. They even serve as politicians' fundraising treasurers. And the amounts at stake are growing, not shrinking.

So what does this mean for lobbying reform? It means that there are limits to what it can accomplish. We may be able to stop a lobbyist from buying dinner for a member of Congress, but we are not going to stop him from throwing a fundraising dinner. We can prohibit a lobbyist from buying a member a fancy tie or a bronze sculpture as a gift, but we cannot stop her from collecting and distributing donations from players in the bronze-sculpture or tie-making industries. There is no law, in other words, that can keep these two powerful forces—politicians seeking money, and lobbyists seeking influence—apart.

What can we do? As I've suggested, we should first resolve to constrain and expose the relationship. Sunshine is a powerful disinfectant, and disclosing the details of members' encounters with lobbyists can make a difference: Who was involved? Whom did they represent? What did they discuss? How much did they spend? How much money did the lobbyists raise for a given politician?

Yet we need to go beyond that. Making sure that the public knows about every dollar spent to affect legislation—through campaign contributions, grassroots lobbying, and public relations campaigns—is crucial. So is placing limits on how campaign money can be collected, with constraints on what lobbyists can raise and distribute. We should not try to rid the campaign system of lobbyists —after all, they have a right to perform their responsibilities—but surely we can keep their activities within bounds. Finally, just as I argued above that it is in the public's interest for the government to fund congressional travel, so I believe it is in our interest to start moving toward some kind of public financing of congressional campaigns in this country, as is already done for presidential campaigns.

For let's be clear what we're talking about: public faith in our representative democracy. Until we can change the culture of money and politics in this country, we are sure to have more scandals, and we will have to work even harder to restore the public confidence that underpins our system of government.

In the End, Responsibility Lies with Politicians and the Voters

This is especially important because of the place that lobbying has come to occupy in the workings of our political system. Regardless of which party controls the White House or Capitol Hill, it has become clear to pretty much every interest imaginable in recent years that Washington can stack the deck in its favor or tilt the field against it, and the lobbying workload has soared as a result. In a very real sense, lobbyists have become intermediaries between Washington and the organizations that represent the vast diversity of people, beliefs, and interests in our society.

With their well-cultivated contacts, lobbyists undoubtedly get the chance to press their cases on Capitol Hill with access that a teacher or farmer could only envy. Yet I don't want to give the impression that "special interests" always overwhelm "the public interest." Lobbyists—at least the best of them—know that what lawmakers want is straightforward, understandable, and accurate information on a given issue. And over the years I have come to know and appreciate the skillful work of many fine and highly professional lobbyists. On any tough policy matter, which will inevitably find Americans coming down on every side of the issue, all the various interests will be armed with good arguments that make the strongest possible case for their position. While it's too simplistic to say that they cancel one another out, this does mean that they serve a useful purpose in helping members of Congress understand an issue and, perhaps even more important, to understand how various constituencies view it.

This suggests a responsibility on the part of public officials who are being lobbied. It is their job not simply to be passive recipients of arguments and information, but to sort through it, and in particular to understand that it comes with a point of view—to listen carefully, in other words, but also remember that a lobbyist presents only one side of a complex issue. The skillful lobbyist, of course, will identify his or her position with the broader public good, but an equally skillful politician understands how to separate the wheat from the rhetorical chaff.

At the same time, ordinary voters should remember that they have one attribute that every member of Congress prizes highly: a vote. For all the campaign contributions they hand out and the access they enjoy, lobbyists don't actually have the final say on whether a member of Congress gets reelected; that's up to the folks back home. Which is why transparency—strict reporting laws on campaign contributions and lobbying expenditures, with easy access to that information for reporters and ordinary Americans—is so important. For in the end, it is the voters who have to judge whether a member of Congress has allowed lobbyists' arguments and contributions to outweigh the interests of his or her constituents and of the public at large.

8

Strengthening Citizen Participation

WHEN I TALK TO GROUPS of people across the country about the need for a stronger Congress, no one disagrees. But we need to transform agreement into action; it takes more than a nodding of heads. With each passing year, I become more impressed with the obligations and responsibilities our form of democracy places upon ordinary people. To put it plainly, our nation depends for its health on the active engagement of its citizens. As Adlai Stevenson once said, "Our government demands, it depends upon, the care and the devotion of the people."[1]

Are the People Prepared?

Every election year, I'm struck by a basic imbalance in media coverage. A great deal of time, space, and attention go to what we should expect from the candidates—on their policy stances, their strengths and weaknesses, their frame of mind at any given moment. Given that voters are called upon to judge the fitness of these politicians to lead this nation, this is understandable.

Yet I can't help but think that something is missing. Such coverage sends an unspoken message that the candidates and their personal qualities are all that matter to our government, which isn't true. There's another part of the equation: the American people. Far too little gets written or broadcast about *our* role in making this democracy work. We ask the candidates whether they're prepared for their responsibilities. We need to ask the same of the American people.

Because we have the oldest enduring republic in the world and a robust ongoing public discourse, it's easy to forget that our system needs constant tending by the people most invested in its success: American citizens. It depends on broad participation in the political process, participation that goes well beyond voting. It depends on an active belief in accommodation and compromise, rather than the winner-take-all single-mindedness that has come to characterize political culture of late. And it depends on a widespread understanding that our system of government gives all of us an *opportunity* to achieve what we want by following paths defined and limited by our Constitution; it does not *guarantee* that we'll get what we want.

Many Americans get discouraged because government works slowly, sometimes frustratingly so. Issues that bedevil society—a failing health-care system, for example, or a poorly performing economy—might not be adequately addressed for years, as the various interests involved hammer at each other in Washington. Our astoundingly diverse nation—each fragment of it with its own beliefs about what is right and wrong—has to find a way of forging an agreement on appropriate policy. This is hard work, and just because Congress and the president don't produce exactly what we want when we want it does not mean that the system is broken, dysfunctional, or even unrepresentative.

To some extent, a more thorough civic education would be helpful here, both in school and afterward. Many Americans' knowledge of basic concepts—the need for a balance of powers at the federal level, or the crucial role compromise plays in making the system work—is weaker than it ought to be. Consultation and accommodation across ideological and party lines, which is how we reach common ground and sustainable solutions, is one of our strengths, not a weakness. Public tolerance for it is crucial. A firm grounding in the fundamentals of American democracy would also build an understanding that final consensus in our system can only rest on extensive deliberation and the input of many different points of view. These are what produce policy that addresses the needs of our people, not the sound bites and spin that Americans too often confuse these days for civic discourse.

Disappointed as people might be with the president or Congress or the Supreme Court, I've never had someone stand up and say, "I don't support the Constitution." There is an inbred respect for our constitutional structure and its system of checks and balances. The challenge for ordinary citizens is to make it work.

This is a challenge for every generation. Our system does not function on automatic pilot. Just because it has worked in the past does not mean we will have a free and successful country in the future. To achieve this, we need a citizenry that not only participates actively, but also expects and encourages each of its members to do so. We need debate, deliberation, accommodation, a healthy system of checks and balances—that includes a strong president and a strong Congress—and an electorate willing to hold those in power accountable when they stray from these basic constitutional principles.

So each election season it's all well and good to inquire aggressively about how well the candidates are prepared for public office. But remember also to turn the inquiry inward and ask how well we are prepared for the obligations of citizenship.

There is no replacement in our system for accepting the responsibility that comes with being an American to help make our system work. It requires skill, patience, and above all an appreciation for the gift given us by our predecessors and a determination not to squander its legacy. So how do we go about ensuring this?

First, We Need an Informed Citizenry

One of the more disturbing pieces of news that came out during the Iraq war was the large number of Americans who believed that Saddam Hussein was involved with the September 11 terrorists. There has never been any evidence for such a link.

You can pass off this widespread belief as simple confusion, or the result of misleading statements by those with a vested interest in pursuing the Iraq war, but it's nothing to be shrugged away. In a democracy, public misperceptions carry an enormous cost.

Consider the federal budget. If you look at polls surveying how Americans think Congress spends their money, you'll find that several sorts of programs top the list. Alongside spending on defense, people often believe that foreign aid or even spending on environmental protection eats up a large proportion of the budget.

This is just wrong. In truth, the largest single portion of the overall federal budget—a full 39 percent of it in 2008—goes to programs for seniors: Social Security, Medicare, and other retirement benefits. This is followed by defense, which gets 22 percent of the budget; welfare, including food stamps and unemployment insurance, at 17 percent; and interest payments on the federal debt, at 7 percent. The environment and foreign aid both check in at one percent. So when someone stands up at a public forum and talks about cutting foreign aid as a way of reducing the budget deficit, the truth is that it wouldn't get us very far.

You could argue, I suppose, that this mismatch between the facts and Americans' beliefs doesn't really matter, so long as their representatives in Congress understand what's what. But it's not a very big step from there to suggesting that we should just forget all this talk of democracy and leave the difficult art of governing in the hands of our betters.

The truth is that for our democracy to work, it needs not just an engaged citizenry, but an informed one. We've known this since this nation's earliest days. The creators of the Massachusetts Constitution of 1780 thought the notion important enough to enshrine it in the state's founding document: "Wisdom and knowledge, as well as virtue, diffused generally among the body of the people," they wrote, are "necessary for the preservation of their rights and liberties."[2]

Getting the basic facts right is essential to governing well. The late Senator Patrick Moynihan put it well when he said to an opponent during a floor debate, "You are entitled to your own opinion, but you are not entitled to your own facts."[3] One of the most critical jobs facing political leaders in a society as complex as ours is to forge a consensus among the many people and interests holding competing views. This is difficult enough to do when everyone agrees on the underlying facts; it is virtually impossible when there is no agreement. Voters' misperceptions, in other words, can become formidable obstacles to the functioning of our system of representative democracy.

These misperceptions develop for many reasons. Public policy is often complex. It can be wearying to sort through all the sources of information—the media, advocacy groups, the internet, politicians, commentators—on any given subject. And there are always political leaders, lobbyists, and others who are willing to let misperceptions linger. After all, if you're opposed ideologically to spending tax dollars on foreign aid, it doesn't hurt your cause if people believe we spend ten or twenty times more on it than we actually do.

By the same token, there is no single fix for the problem. Part of the answer lies with members of Congress and other public officials, who should feel great responsibility to correct public misperceptions when they surface. Part of it lies with the media, which in recent years has shown a worrisome tendency to downplay its role as even-handed, in-depth civic educator and focus instead on entertainment or once-over-lightly reporting. Part of it lies with civic groups—some of them do their level best to counter the flood of misinformation, but they often seem entirely outmatched.

In the end, though, the burden lies with each of us citizens. There are a lot of powerful groups and interests in this country that try to manipulate public opinion, and they're very good at it. Yet a democratic society depends on the ability of its citizens to separate the fact from the fiction, to form good judgments, and to put pressure on their representatives to act accordingly. If ordinary people can't do this or don't want to devote the time and energy to it, the country suffers. No matter how good our leadership, if we don't have discriminating citizens, this nation will not work very well. There is an old observation that a society of sheep must in time beget a government of wolves. Living in a democracy may be a basic right, but it is also a privilege, and it is one that must be earned by living up to the fondest dreams of our founders for a well-educated and knowledgeable citizenry.

"If a nation expects to be ignorant and free, in a state of civilization, it expects what never was and never will be," Thomas Jefferson once wrote to a friend.[4] Our first duties may be to our families and our immediate communities, but our freedom depends on the willingness of ordinary citizens to devote time, attention, and effort to the public interest as well.

We Also Need a Citizenry That Looks for Candidates Who Respect Congress

Given the media's fascination with the race for the White House, it's easy to forget in presidential election years that contests are also taking place for all 435 U.S. House seats and a third of the 100 seats in the U.S. Senate. Unfortunately, in those many congressional contests the candidates and press rarely talk about one of the most important issues we face as a nation: the role of Congress itself.

The litany of matters worrying Americans and absorbing the attention of congressional candidates is, of course, long and complex: the economy, the wars in Iraq and Afghanistan, the challenges posed by Iran, the state of American public education, climate change, a long-term energy policy, immigration . . . Not surprisingly, many voters want to hear how Congress can protect them from financial ruin or how candidates propose to keep America strong.

Yet unless Congress learns how to reassert its constitutional responsibility to be the president's equal in policy making, the progress voters yearn to see on all those issues will be much harder to come by. This is why, as you listen to the various House and Senate candidates campaigning for your vote, I hope you'll pay attention not only to what they say about the economy or Iraq, but to how they talk about Congress itself.

It's been the habit of both incumbents and their challengers in recent years to run for Congress by running against the Congress. They criticize its profligate spending or its do-nothing ways or its shoddy ethics or the undue influence of money and lobbyists, and they say that *they* are the candidate who can clean up the mess in Washington. These are all choice targets, and they have their place in the campaign debate, but you have to wonder how long this denigration of Congress can continue before Americans lose their faith in representative democracy.

There's another path, and that's to recognize that Congress is flawed but that, as an institution, it needs to be upheld and shored up, not stigmatized. As I've argued, a robust, functional, and assertive Congress is crucial to making our system work. It must be able to keep an eye on the executive branch, advance an agenda based on its members' understanding of what the country needs, be the place where the cross-currents roiling the American community meet in constructive debate, and in general play the muscular role our founders envisioned for it in policy making. It cannot do any of these things if it is filled with politicians who are adept at making themselves look good and the Congress look bad, or who care little about its institutional powers.

I've noticed something interesting as I have moved around the country recently: people are starting to catch on to this. They express disappointment that Congress for decades has allowed the White House to dominate it. They fret that the expansion of presidential power pursued by the George W. Bush administration went too far, and are bewildered by Congress's timidity in asserting its own powers. This is an extremely promising development—if it translates into an electorate willing to look carefully at how congressional candidates propose to set Congress back on track, and if it begins to wake up Congress as a whole.

For make no mistake, this is not just a matter of political theory or a topic for a good speech on the importance of constitutional checks and balances. It has to be practiced in the day-to-day workings of Capitol Hill. If you ask candidates whether they are in favor of reasserting congressional authority, the answer will almost certainly be yes. But that's not enough.

What you also want to know is whether they'll be aggressive in shaping the federal budget; whether they believe Congress has a strong voice, along with the president's, in declaring war or pursuing military intervention overseas; whether they'll work with their colleagues to develop and fight for Congress's own agenda, and not simply respond to the president's; whether they see that getting Congress's ethical house in order is crucial to building its institutional strength, not just a matter of political expediency; whether they understand that Congress must be a truly deliberative and consensus-building body, not a place where the majority ramrods its wishes through without debate; and whether they understand that violating long-standing and fair procedure—by passing sprawling omnibus bills, for instance—merely hands the president more power.

If they get all this, even if they don't share your views on a few policy issues, then you and our country would be ably served by their presence in Washington.

Why Political Virtue Matters

When Americans talk about what kind of people they like to have representing them in Washington, personal integrity is high on the list, above almost any other trait. Most of us also want to know that the people to whom we entrust our hopes for this nation aren't just in it for themselves.

The Founding Fathers would approve. Indeed, they were quite clear on which particular quality they thought most important in our elected representatives: virtue. It's an old-fashioned word that is not much in vogue at the moment, yet in a very real sense, the vitality of our democracy depends on what the Founders meant by it.

People today might think of "virtue" in any number of ways: as moral probity, honesty, self-discipline, a sense of responsibility, and, of course, integrity. These are all qualities that citizens want in their representatives, and understandably so. Yet the Founders had something even larger and more encompassing in mind when they talked about virtue. They were looking for a sense of civic self-sacrifice—the ability to overcome self-interest and act for the benefit of the broader community.

There is nothing anachronistic about "virtue" when seen in that light. Our republic functions best when it generates political leaders who are capable of setting aside their own desires for power or partisan domination or pecuniary self-interest, and it suffers when our politicians are incapable of doing so.

Of course, the Founders also understood human nature. They anticipated that no one could be so virtuous that he or she could be entrusted with unlimited power. That is why they developed a constitutional system of checks and balances aimed at restraining the power of any single person or, indeed, any branch of government.

Yet the Founders were keenly aware that even this was not enough. They were creating a representative democracy, and in a democracy, power ultimately lies with the electorate. In 1788, at the Virginia Ratifying Convention, James Madison laid out what this meant: "I go on this great republican principle," he said, "that the people will have virtue and intelligence to select men of virtue and wisdom. Is there no virtue among us? If there be not, we are in a wretched situation . . . To suppose that any form of government will secure liberty or happiness without any virtue in the people, is a chimerical idea."[5]

The ultimate check, in other words, would be the American people. In order to preserve our freedoms they, too, must be virtuous—at least, in the civic sense that the Founders had in mind. As the historian Bernard Bailyn put it, "an informed, alert, intelligent, and uncorrupted electorate" is vital to sustaining the American republic. George Washington, Bailyn once wrote, believed "that the guarantee that the American government would never degenerate into despotism lay in the ultimate virtue of the American people."[6]

This faith—that man possesses sufficient virtue for self-government—is hardly something to take for granted. The Founders never envisioned the dark arts of modern politicking: the insistence that what is good for me is good for everyone; the evasive answer to an uncomfortable question; the efforts we've seen in recent elections to suppress voter turnout; the television advertising that misleads without actually lying; the "spin" put on the facts by a political operation. Nor could they have foreseen the pressures that make it difficult for members of Congress and other political leaders to step back and disentangle what is best for the country from their more personal preoccupations: the high-stakes gamesmanship of politics today; the influence of campaign contributions; the complexity and sheer quantity of legislation; the bewildering clamor of different voices and divergent needs that confront any lawmaker.

Under these circumstances, the responsibility that the Founders laid on the American people weighs more heavily than ever: to pay attention, to discern insincerity and reject misinformation, to enter the voting booth prepared to set aside one's own self-interest and focus on the good of the country. None of this is easy. Yet that is precisely the expectation that the founders of this nation bore for the generations that followed them: that the American people not only would choose leaders of wisdom and virtue, but would themselves possess the intelligence and virtue to do so. Let us hope we never prove them wrong.

The Ten Commandments of Good Citizenship

Everyone is talking now about change in Washington, and how we want our political leaders to bring it about. It is the cause of the moment, and expectations are high. Yet I have news for you: change in Washington won't happen, and certainly can't be sustained, without change in the country at large. For the point is not to overthrow the system, it's to make it function properly. Government does not fix itself. Only a citizenry that is engaged in our democracy to an extent far greater than in recent decades can help to heal our system. To get change in Washington, in other words, it has to begin with you.

Since being a responsible citizen takes commitment, here are some precepts to follow if you want to be effective—what I call "The Ten Commandments of Good Citizenship." Some involve what citizens should do, others what citizens should understand:

1. *Vote.* This is the most basic step democracy asks of us. Don't buy the argument that it doesn't matter. Every election offers real choices about the direction we want our towns, states, and country to take. By voting, you not only select the officials who will run the government, you suggest the direction government policy should take and reaffirm your support for a representative democracy.

2. *Be informed.* To be a knowledgeable voter, you need to know what candidates actually stand for, not just what their ads or their opponents' ads say. Read about the issues that confront your community and our nation as a whole. Our government simply does not work well if its citizens are ill-informed.

3. *Communicate with your representatives.* Representative democracy is a dialogue between elected officials and citizens—that dialogue lies at the heart of our system. Legislators and executives can't do their job well if they don't understand their constituents' concerns, and we can't understand them if we don't know their views and why they hold them.

4. *Participate in groups that share your views and can advance your interests.* This one's simple: in a democracy, people tend to be more effective when they work together than as individuals. You can be sure that almost every issue you care about has one or more organizations devoted to it. By joining and working with the ones you think best reflect your views, you amplify your beliefs and strengthen the dialogue of democracy.

5. *Get involved locally to improve your community.* You know more about your community's strengths and weaknesses than anyone living outside it. Identify its problems and work to correct them. Involvement is the best antidote I know to cynicism.

6. *Educate your family, and make sure that local schools are educating students, about their responsibilities as citizens.* As a society, we're not as good as we should be at encouraging young people to get involved in political life. Too many young people will become adults without understanding how our government and political system work and why it is important for them to be contributing citizens.

7. *Understand that we must work to build consensus in a huge, diverse country.* In pretty much every way you can think of, ours is an astoundingly mixed nation of people, with wildly divergent views on most issues and a constantly growing population. This means we have to work through our differences not by hammering on the other side, but by bringing people together through the arts of dialogue, accommodation, compromise, and consensus building.

8. *Understand that our representative democracy works slowly.* There's a reason for this: it is so that all sides can be heard, and so that we avoid the costly mistakes produced by haste. Our founders understood this 220 years ago, and it's even more vital now, when issues are vastly more complex and the entire world is closely connected.

9. *Understand that our system is not perfect but has served the nation well.* Democracy is a process designed to give people a voice in how they are governed. It's not perfect—far too many people feel voiceless, and polls in recent years suggest that unsettling numbers believe the system is broken. And our system offers no guarantee that you'll get what you want. Yet it is also true that it provides every individual an opportunity to be heard and to work to achieve his or her objectives, and it has served our nation well for over two centuries.

10. *Understand that our system is not self-perpetuating; it demands our involvement to survive.* Just because it has worked in the past

does not mean we will have a free and successful country in the future. Lincoln's challenge at Gettysburg is still urgent: whether this "government of the people, by the people, for the people" can long endure. Being a good citizen isn't something one does just for the heck of it; it's critical to the success of our nation.

9

A Well-Functioning Congress

THE NEWLY REVITALIZED, stronger Congress that I've envisioned in these pages would certainly be a better counterbalance to the president on matters like the federal budget and the decision to go to war, and it would be a more vigorous representative of the American people than in the past. But how should it function? What should we expect from such a Congress? And above all, how would it actually work to further the national good? A well-functioning Congress—a Congress that is a fuller partner in our representative democracy—will have several core characteristics. This chapter identifies nine.

It Will Search for Remedy

Over the years, I've met with a lot of high school and college students, and there's one question they come up with time after time. What, they want to know, is politics really about?

Having spent a good part of my life in the trenches, I long ago arrived at an answer that I thought reflected reality and was sufficiently cynical to make me believable. Politics, I would tell them, is about power: getting it, keeping it, and using it to advance one's agenda.

At least that's what I said until I ran across a comment by the late historian Arthur Schlesinger, Jr. He had a different, and far more useful, answer. Politics is about "the search for remedy," he said.[1]

We live at a time when such a belief seems outdated and hopelessly earnest. Americans have watched their politicians over the years with increasing skepticism, and come to the belief that politics is about anything but an honest effort to resolve the issues that confront us. It's about personal egos. It's about enriching oneself. It's about winning elections or wielding power for its own sake.

What's disheartening is that politicians themselves have contributed to this abandonment of sincerity. Often they—and especially their consultants—talk about politics as a highly technical and fascinating game whose largest purpose is to experience the thrill of victory. In a gubernatorial primary a few years back, the advertising of one leading candidate ended in the tagline "The only Republican who can win in November." Don't get me wrong; electability is hardly irrelevant to a primary voter. But should that be our sole measure of a political leader?

What Schlesinger invited us to do was to search beneath the definitions we've given politics over the years and find an underlying purpose. All those "abouts" you hear now—it's about ego, it's about money, it's about power—are partly true, or true in certain cases. But they're inadequate when it comes to describing what politics in a democracy is truly about. Politics is how we wrestle with and try to resolve the challenges that confront us.

To see why this is so important, think for a moment about some of the tremendously difficult issues we face. For years in Washington, there was constant finger-pointing and ex post facto analysis of what went wrong in Iraq. This had its place, if only because we should learn from our mistakes, but seen through the lens of Schlesinger's formulation it was a political sideshow. The real challenge was to devise a remedy that Congress and the White House could embrace and implement. That was what true politicians spent their time on.

So, too, with our health-care system. Until President Obama launched his health-care initiative, there hadn't been an all-out effort to reform the system since the failure of President Bill Clinton's plan over a decade ago. The result is that the system has grown more expensive, more wasteful, and less helpful to growing numbers of Americans. It is a situation that calls for politics at its best, an honest and concerted effort to find a remedy that not only is fair and lasting, but can win the support of a diverse nation.

You'll notice that in both these examples I've added something to Schlesinger's phrase: that solutions have to be pragmatic and broadly acceptable. If politics at heart is a means to an end—the end being an actual fix to a problem—then it is not just about the search for an answer, but about making that answer work.

This means that the best politicians don't just dream up policy solutions regardless of context. They also think about how those solutions would work in the real world; they think about the forces that can help them and those that can block them; and perhaps above all, they think about how to build the broadest consensus possible behind their solutions, so that they have a realistic chance of taking root and flourishing.

So as you keep your eye on Washington, I'd ask you to keep Schlesinger in mind. Are your representatives in Congress interested in constructive problem solving? Are they engaged wholeheartedly in "the search for remedy"? Do they act as though they understand that Congress has a crucial role to play in this process?

It Will Look Ahead

Much of the debate after the terrorist attacks of September 11, 2001, focused on the shortsightedness revealed within executive-branch circles and federal intelligence agencies. There is another branch of government, though, whose failings ought to have alarmed us as well: Congress.

It may seem odd to say this. Is it really Congress's job to protect American soil from attack? The answer, of course, is no, not directly. But it *is* Congress's job to make sure that the federal government as a whole is on top of its game, alert to problems that could be coming at us in the future. Yet in the years just before the 9/11 attacks, even though members of Congress knew that terrorism was a threat to U.S. interests, hearings to look into the matter were modest and episodic. When intelligence briefings took place to discuss the dangers, they were sparsely attended. Congress, too, was caught unprepared.

This is not an isolated example. The fact is, Congress is not very good at looking ahead. It falls especially short when it comes to identifying issues that do not cause any immediate problem, but that, if left unattended, might some day rear up and bite us. Congress did not give enough attention to the warning signs for the housing bubble, the Wall Street meltdown, or the energy crunch—in fact, a speech I gave in the 1970s on the need for energy independence could be repeated today almost word for word. Our nation's aging and deteriorating infrastructure gets attention only after a major bridge collapses. We have heard for years about how the Social Security and Medicare trust funds will be depleted during the baby boomers' retirement, yet the first wave of baby boomers is starting to retire now.

Other challenges loom on the horizon. Over the last few years, for instance, Congress has essentially ignored the growing income inequality in this country that has concentrated an astounding percentage of private wealth in fewer and fewer hands; not only has it failed to examine its own role in creating this situation, it has shown no interest at all in the political and economic repercussions should most Americans come to decide that the system is stacked against them. Insufficient attention has also been given to the large number of children in America living in poverty, the depletion of our nation's freshwater supplies, the availability of food worldwide, and the emergence of new strands of disease that are resistant to treatment. All of these are potentially huge problems, yet Congress seems largely uninterested.

Why would this be? For one thing, there's not much immediate political benefit to examining the far horizon for approaching storms. Members of Congress are quite attuned to the immediate concerns of their constituents; anyone who spent too much of his or her time investigating long-term global water supplies would no doubt hear about it at the next round of town hall meetings. Then, too, the close partisan divide within the country as a whole has made it difficult for Congress to move forward even on the issues it does address. The result is that members are under great pressure to focus on immediate issues that might give their side some advantage at the polls. There is much truth in the observation that Congress cannot look beyond the next election.

Yet this is an area in which the Congress could make a major contribution, and, indeed, is particularly suited for. Congress was designed to proceed slowly, cautiously, deliberatively—to prevent rash responses and to provide many opportunities for input and review along the way. That measured pace might not be best for immediate crises that need quick policy responses, but it does work well for focusing on serious long-term challenges: it gives all sides a chance to be heard and allows legislators to examine an issue from every angle, understand its intricacies, look for unforeseen and unintended consequences, build consensus on Capitol Hill, educate the American people as to what needs to be done and why, and create support in the country at large. Getting the American people to go along with the steps needed to put Social Security and Medicare on durable footing, for example, would require nothing less.

Congress has the capacity to focus more on the long term; it just needs the political will. Our country faces so many challenges that as a nation we can ill afford to have an entire branch of government wrapped up in short-term political thinking. As Thomas Jefferson put it, we need to lengthen our horizon to how our actions would affect the "thousandth generation."

Over the last few decades, Congress has grown increasingly accustomed to thinking of itself as an adjunct to the president, reduced in stature by its desire to help him when it is controlled by the same party, and by its determination to jab at him when it is not. Yet with so many deep-rooted challenges looming, the interests of our nation demand a different understanding of what Congress is about. Congress needs to take a major role in exploring in a deliberative way the wide-ranging and potentially very serious challenges facing our country, so that we can understand their causes, evaluate their possible consequences, and examine policies that might begin to address them now in a responsible, prudent way.

It Will Help to Set the Agenda

The inauguration of President Barack Obama was a groundbreaking event, but in one way his presidency began like the others before it: every four years, after a long campaign in which two rivals trade policy prescriptions and accusations about their respective flaws, the country eagerly awaits the agenda of the new president. For the public, Congress remains largely an afterthought, its views given weight only insofar as they might hinder or abet the president's plans.

And really, why should they matter? The 435 House members and 100 senators present a cacophony of views—they're liberal and conservative, from large states and small, representing every conceivable kind of American voter. It's impossible for them to speak with one voice or with the institutional heft to be found at the other end of Pennsylvania Avenue.

Moreover, Congress long ago abandoned the practice of trying to put forward in a major way its own plans, and Americans have certainly lost the habit of looking to it for leadership. Even *Congressional Quarterly,* a magazine whose reason for being is to parse every nuance of life on Capitol Hill, titled its cover story a month before the 2008 election "11 Issues for the Next President." It went on to say, "The winner of the Nov. 4 election will face the most difficult roster of top-tier issues in a generation while trying to restore the country's faith in its government."[2] On everything from the economy to taxes, energy, and our nation's infrastructure needs, it suggested, Congress would be left to react, not to create.

While this picture certainly fits our national expectations, there are two problems with it: it's not how things are supposed to be; and it's not healthy for the United States. The Constitution sets out a very clear expectation that Congress and the president are to be colleagues—equals—in determining the course of the country. There is a compelling reason for this: the very forces that make it difficult for Congress to speak with one voice, especially its members' closeness to the diverse constituencies from which they hail, also provide Congress with a fine-textured understanding of national concerns and sentiment. Better than any other part of the federal government, Congress reflects the regional, ideological, economic, and cultural diversity of the United States.

This is crucial to crafting good policy, policy that is consistent, relevant, and sustainable over the long term. Such policy springs not from a single opinion about what's needed, but from sharp analysis and civil dialogue among people with different points of view, values, and experiences. Congress, in other words, is as indispensable as the president in laying out a national policy agenda.

Because it has chosen not to play that role in recent decades—with a few exceptions—it has turned into a reactive body with very little control over the policy debate; he who sets the agenda, after all, controls the discussion and usually the results, and recent presidents have been extremely forceful about putting forth both a domestic and a foreign agenda for the nation. It has been politically easier for members of Congress to let the president take the lead, especially since it is hard work to craft an agenda that a majority of both houses can agree upon.

Given this history and the atrophy of Congress's policy-crafting muscles, it seems unreasonable to expect that Congress will suddenly set about advancing its own agenda for every problem, foreign and domestic, that confronts us. Yet surely it's in a position to act more forcefully than it has in the recent past. If it wishes to fulfill its constitutional role and rebuild its standing as an institution that commands the respect of the American people—and, more important, that earns legitimacy as a branch of government—it should start to put forward initiatives to which the president can respond. Congress needs to be a more assertive presence in Washington generally, and it certainly needs to flex its policy-making muscles more frequently than it does now.

How might it do so? The party caucuses in each house—that is, the meetings at which Democrats and Republicans gather to work on their own marching orders—are the appropriate place to start. Democrats in Congress ought to see it as their responsibility to put forward their own agenda for the nation, not one that largely reacts to the president's; Republicans should too. The parties might even find some common ground. And in the debates over what these agendas should be, and then in the conversation with the White House that will surely result, Congress might just find its own voice. That would be a good thing not only for its members, but for us all.

It Will Give Voice to a Diverse People

Of course, if you watch Congress in action, you sometimes can't help but wonder whether it can ever find a single voice. It quarrels not just over the big, divisive issues like the Iraq war, the automobile industry bailout, and what sort of energy policy should guide the nation, but in any number of other dustups and outright policy brawls that seem to take place every time you look in on a committee room or chamber on Capitol Hill.

A lot of people don't like this. Pretty much every time I address an audience, someone complains, "I'm sick and tired of all the bickering. Those guys are always fighting." And everyone will nod.

Most people are uncomfortable with disagreement and debate. As individuals, this is fine; but as citizens, I would argue that we should not only get used to it, we should be pleased by it. It has been a constant in American politics, and let us hope it always will be.

Extensive debate is built into the very structure of our congressional system. At every level, from subcommittees through committees to the floor of each chamber and then to the conference committees that bring members from each house of Congress together, it is presumed that discussion, debate, disagreement, and even altercation will take place. Our founders understood the importance of conflict in the system, both as a way for all views to be represented and as a process for building common ground among those holding divergent views.

For the fundamental fact of our democracy is that Americans, despite all that unites us, nonetheless have much that divides us: different philosophies, different prospects in life, different backgrounds, different communities, and different ways of defining what is in our own interest, what is in our community's interest, and what is in our nation's best interest. Take the issue of immigration reform. For some, illegal immigration is a scourge that must be dealt with harshly; for others, it's a fact of life that requires us to integrate millions of people into our society; for still others, immigration presents an opportunity to build an economy for the twenty-first century.

It's true that our divisions can be exacerbated by special interests, the media, and politicians all seeking to exploit them for their own ends, but that doesn't mean the initial disagreements don't exist. They do. And it is Congress's job to give voice to all our differences and then sort through them as it strives to find the majorities it needs to move forward on legislation that serves the national interest. If there weren't conflict, it wouldn't be doing its job.

There are certainly times when the conflict built into our system gets out of hand, and the people involved become mean-spirited or angry. But overall, disputation and debate are not a weakness of our democracy, they're a strength. They lead to better, more sustainable decisions. They help build majority support for a proposal.

And they are part of how we talk to one another as we search for common ground.

Some issues are extremely difficult to resolve. They take years of wrangling, arguing, and debate simply for members to find enough in common that they can move forward. It helps to look past the often messy process and judge Congress by the end results. Whether to increase the minimum wage, how best to shape our homeland security system, whether to protect wilderness areas—all of these have been subject to heartfelt and sometimes quite contentious disputes over the years, but in the end, Congress reaches a conclusion and we move on.

Indeed, I believe that we are stronger for the sometimes difficult road Congress has to travel as it searches for solutions to the challenges that confront us. For a strong debate means that all sides get a chance to be heard and have their arguments weighed, and that helps to prevent excessive concentration of power. Keep in mind that the most efficient and debate-free political system is a dictatorship.

So let's not expect Congress to be free of contention. The better approach is to manage the debate so it is civil, inclusive, serious, and constructive. Giving all sides a chance to voice their views is not only what Congress is supposed to do, it helps to resolve differences. Yes, Congress sometimes has trouble managing all these strongly held views, but that is far preferable to a system that allows for no conflict at all.

It Will Forge Consensus

Still, this is why—especially in challenging and divisive times—the single most important political skill for a member of Congress to have is the ability to build consensus. That may not get the most attention in the national media or when local citizens discuss what they're looking for in candidates. But making progress in Washington on the important issues before the country means hammering out solutions that can command broad support in a deeply divided country. That's not easy, and we need politicians who can do it.

Our country is closely divided ideologically, with political parties and their adherents ready to scrap over every vote at the polls and every issue that comes before the Congress. Yet if we are to successfully tackle the daunting challenges we face, it will be because political leaders manage to overcome the forces that divide us. In the current political environment, narrow legislative majorities do not build sustainable policies—solutions that enjoy support among the population at large and legitimacy among the array of policy makers who must sign off on them.

Building consensus on Capitol Hill, however, is about the toughest, most thankless job in politics. To begin with, the sheer number and complexity of the issues we face means that it is hard for any single politician to devote the sustained time and attention it takes to gather facts and opinions about a problem, listen to the concerns of the various interests involved, spend time discoursing with colleagues who have opposing views, work with them to find steps they can agree upon, bring in other politicians and interest groups to form a supportive coalition, and then build majority support in Congress. Assaulted by the Iraq war, concerns about the readiness of the U.S. military, constituents losing their homes, crisis in the financial industry, failing national infrastructure, an unsustainable health-care system, and a plethora of other issues, lawmakers can barely manage to keep abreast of them all, let alone work to find broad-based solutions.

When Congress does focus on a particular problem, the politics quickly becomes tangled. Because our country is diverse in so many different ways, it is rare to find solid majorities in favor of a given approach. Public opinion may support the notion that manmade climate change is real and that governments need to address it, for instance, but that's where the agreement ends—and where lawmakers' work begins. Moreover, Washington is full of skilled and often well-funded lobbyists whose job is to make sure their points of view are vigorously represented at all stages of the legislative process. Because the stakes are so high and so much money is at risk on most issues, legislators often find themselves pulled in half a dozen different directions, making consensus even more difficult to forge.

All of this can be overcome, but it takes time, care, and a fundamental willingness on the part of legislative leaders and ordinary members to achieve it. All of these are in short supply right now. Members' schedules are so full that the chance for thoughtful deliberation is rare; there's precious little time for the extended conversations and interplay of ideas that produce compromise and agreement. Nor is there much desire. Years of partisan wrangling and tit-for-tat political maneuvering have left Democrats and Republicans wary of one another, unwilling to share credit, always searching for ways to discredit the other side, and interested more in avoiding blame for problems than in setting aside their disagreements to work together on devising solutions.

Yet survey after survey indicates that Americans want their elected leaders to work across party lines. My work on the 9/11 Commission reinforced my sense that the basics of building consensus are fairly straightforward, at least in theory: Work cooperatively, not confrontationally. Look at your colleagues as partners rather than political adversaries. Agree on facts before you apply your ideology to policy. Take ample time to understand different views. Search for areas of agreement, and do not exaggerate areas of disagreement. Get people focused on the national interest, not on partisan advantage. And decide from the start that you're going to reach an agreement rather than use disagreement to score political points. Carrying all this out, of course, is not as easy as it sounds. But it is doable.

Certainly, building consensus is not always necessary to making policy. When I first arrived in Congress, when Lyndon Johnson was president and his Great Society was being formulated, he and his party had significant majorities in both the House and the Senate as well as widespread political backing among voters that enabled them to enact in a matter of weeks Medicare, federal aid to education, and the like. Devoting a lot of time to building consensus was not necessary.

Now, however, narrow congressional majorities, stark political divisions, the echo chamber of partisanship, the huge stakes that attend every battle for power—all make it very difficult, if not impossible, to enact responsible and lasting policies by overwhelming the opposition. Building consensus may be difficult, but in today's political environment it is the only realistic course.

In his book about America's fifty greatest legislative achievements over the past half century, the political scientist Paul Light concluded that these major accomplishments "reflect a stunning level of bipartisan commitment." The GI Bill, the Marshall Plan, welfare reform in the 1990s—all involved considerable bipartisan legwork. Greatness in policy making, in other words, usually requires great effort in consensus building.[3]

That road to making good policy can be fraught and difficult, yet I'm reminded of Gerald Ford's comment when he became president after Richard Nixon's resignation: "The Constitution works," he said. It does. We might not always enjoy the troubles that assail us along the way, but in the end we move past the difficulty of the moment, work together to achieve at least a few victories, and, refreshed, square our shoulders to face the next challenge.

It Will Exercise Judgment

I'm a firm believer in the political arts. The ability to read the mood of an electorate, an aptitude for building consensus among competing interests, a gift for finding just the right tack for eliciting people's agreement—these talents are indispensable to making Congress and our democracy work.

Yet lately I've also wondered whether politics as we practice it today is working as well as it should. In some ways, politicians are acting too much like politicians for the country's good.

To understand this, let's step back for a moment and remember the difference between a representative democracy, which is the system we live in, and a direct democracy. As it is now, we elect people to represent us and to make decisions about the issues confronting us that, ideally, will make ours a better and stronger nation. If we lived in a pure, direct democracy, we'd be making those decisions ourselves.

Any politician will tell you there is a great deal of wisdom and common sense to be found in the American electorate. Time and again I've been impressed by the comments of people I've met with from all walks of life and all backgrounds. Yet we live in a representative democracy for a reason: the Founders who designed our system wanted to reserve a place for deliberation, study, and thoroughgoing argument. They worried that popular majorities could be swayed by the passions of the moment or by self-interest, rather than by carefully reasoned debate about where the best interests of the country might lie.

Fast-forward to today, and you'll notice that while we still live in a representative democracy, our representatives too often seem to be guided by polls of their constituents or by the desires of interests that have their ear. There are times when it seems as though the one thing our system was designed to ensure—that our representatives would think hardest about what's good for the country as they weigh the issues before them—is the last thing on their minds.

What we need are politicians who understand their responsibility both to reflect the popular will *and* to educate and lead the public—who, in essence, recognize that in a representative democracy, the people elect them to use their judgment and steer by their own convictions. Good politicians see their job as building consensus for pragmatic and effective policies through deliberation and accommodation; they are not simple weather vanes, shifting this way or that according to the views contained in the latest polls or the advice of their favorite political consultant. We hear much today in politics about the search for "authenticity" in political candidates; this is, I believe, a reflection of Americans' desire for political leaders who understand that while good leadership begins with listening, it cannot end there.

Getting the balance right between reflecting the views of the American people and allowing for the judgment and skill of the elected representative is difficult. But it is hard for me to imagine that a politician who focuses on what is best for our country can go too far wrong. A clash between enlightened politicians who are determined to find remedies that serve the public good will almost certainly produce better policy than politicians who view their job as mirroring the latest polls.

It Will Be Led Responsibly

One key to almost everything I've outlined above—and, indeed, to whether Congress can reach its potential as a representative body equal in weight to the presidency—will be the congressional leadership. These individuals set the tone of the Congress. They can act as stewards of its institutional strength, integrity, and effectiveness, or squander its potential. They signal how much weight they'll attach to ethical behavior and tough ethics enforcement, and they can make or break legislation designed to further it. They determine whether cooperation across party lines will be the order of the day, a rarity, or out of the question. They decide how the budget is to be put together. Above all, they craft the congressional agenda and determine whether it's going to be used merely to score political points or to respond in good faith to challenges facing our nation.

Leaders are in a position to determine which issues will come forward for consideration, and which will be set aside; what oversight will be done and what ignored; what will get the media spotlight and what will remain in the shadows; which programs will be included in appropriations bills and which won't. They have enormous power, in other words, over both the substance and the style of Congress. And they are the ones who largely determine whether Congress will become a stronger partner in our representative democracy or will continue to defer to the president.

In some periods, as during the Great Society era in the 1960s, Congress was highly regarded because it was seen as addressing the key problems facing the country. There were significant accomplishments amid bipartisan cooperation, if not collegiality. Other periods have seen a breakdown on both fronts. And still others may produce a less productive record on legislation, but still be marked by an overall respect for the Congress's integrity as an institution. When House Speaker Tip O'Neill and Minority Leader Bob Michel squared off in public debate during the 1980s, for instance, it was only after intense but congenial discussions over how each of their caucuses viewed a measure; they would give a ringing speech on the floor to rally their troops, but in almost every case each man knew how the vote would turn out. They knew how to work with one another to ensure that Congress lived up to its constitutional responsibilities, while remaining true to their political responsibilities.

Leaders must be held principally responsible for the performance of the Congress. If the institution is not performing well under stress—if it is ignoring proper budget process, sidestepping tough issues, not disciplining wayward members, or deferring excessively to the president and neglecting its constitutional role—that is a failure of congressional leadership. Often, leaders are quick to blame the opposition for standing in the way of progress, and sometimes that's legitimate; frequently, though, it's because the leaders failed to work well together, putting political advantage over legislative solutions.

Over the last few decades, the leaders' responsibility for Congress's performance has grown measurably greater. This is because their power has, too. Leaders of both parties have worked to increase their budgets and concentrate power in their offices. Their staffs have grown—where a Speaker or minority leader might once have turned for policy advice to the chairs of particular committees, they now have their own advisers on energy or foreign policy or the economy. And they have changed the process to favor themselves, most notably with the budget. When spending priorities were put together by the various committees, rank-and-file members knew in detail what was in the budget and they had significant input into its contents. Now, Congress often acts by omnibus bill, which puts enormous power in the hands of a few leaders and their staff.

This has not been a favorable trend. While strong, effective leaders are necessary for restoring Congress to its position as a co-equal branch of government, concentrating too much power in the hands of the leadership can diminish the role of other members and distort representative democracy. Congress derives its legitimacy and authority from its members, who represent the American people in all their diversity. This is why the Framers put Congress first in the Constitution. For Congress to assert its standing as a separate, independent, and forceful branch of government, that multitude of voices needs to be heard.

It Will Engage in Genuine Consultation

Here I want to reiterate a point I made earlier in this book. When I say that Congress needs to be stronger and more assertive, that doesn't mean it should adopt a hard-line approach with the president, fighting him tooth and nail at every turn.

Disagreements over policy between the White House and Congress are inevitable. But they need not become all-or-nothing battles, which too often result in nothing being accomplished to advance public policy. Governing well is not about hammering at the other side until it relents; it's about working hard to find whatever common ground is possible. It means both sides making greater efforts to consult and negotiate with each other.

The key point about governing and consultation between the two branches of government is that it has to be sincere—a true effort to engage and work with the other branch in the decision-making process. It doesn't work for the president and his advisers to call in the congressional leadership, announce a decision that has already been made, and call that "consultation." It's equally unproductive for a congressional majority to gamble that it will be rewarded in the court of electoral opinion for excluding White House input from its bills. To bridge the differences, there must be a very strong will to succeed. What's needed is a process that creates an ongoing relationship—not just one to deal with an immediate crisis—that builds trust among the various players, recognizes that there are always alternatives in policy disputes, and allows key negotiators to sit down and talk long before decisions are made.

Not only does this work to both sides' political advantage, it usually produces better policy for the American people. I'm reminded, for instance, of the intensive negotiations between Secretary of State George Marshall and Senator Arthur Vandenberg of Michigan that produced the Marshall Plan for the reconstruction of postwar Europe, despite the general state of suspicion between the Republican-held Congress and the White House of President Harry Truman, a Democrat. Or President George H. W. Bush's efforts to convince a dubious Congress to allocate large amounts of financial aid to Eastern Europe and the former Soviet Union after the fall of communism; rather than try to bludgeon Congress into going along, he involved Congress in designing the aid programs. Or the long, tedious, contentious discussions between any White House and Congress on just about any major piece of legislation, from aid to education to welfare reform, that has resulted in an advance in public policy.

By its nature, Congress represents the diversity of the American people and articulates their concerns. Yet only rarely can Congress hope to enact policy over the president's veto; it cannot change the course of American policy without him. And a president usually cannot get what he wants just by flexing his muscle.

Our system relies on creative tension between a strong Congress and a strong president for the simple reason that different opinions and approaches, forthrightly stated and creatively resolved, produce the best policy. So to govern effectively, the two branches need to work with, not against, one another. Consultation is hardly a confession of political weakness: it's a pragmatic recognition that in our system, the two branches need to talk to one another.

It Will Seek the Common Good

I want to conclude with a moment that has stuck with me for many years now. It was election day, and I was back in the southern Indiana district I represented in Congress, making the rounds of voting precincts and chatting with voters. Outside, I ran into an older woman I'd never met before and asked her whether she'd voted. She said she had, and then added, "You know, I vote for my candidate, and then I go home and pray for the winner." I asked her what she meant. "Well, I want him or her to work not just for a few," she said, "but for everyone."

I never did meet that woman again, but I have never forgotten our encounter. In that brief comment, I thought, she expressed the healthiest attitude toward politics I'd ever heard, and said it better than any politician or pundit. I think it's what most of us want: that our elected representatives work not just for a few, but for everyone.

Congress doesn't do it enough: it does not focus sufficiently on the common good. There are lots of reasons for this, some of them quite understandable. As a member of Congress, for instance, you might have fifteen meetings a day and every single one will be with someone who wants his or her slice of the federal budget. There are farmers and small-business people and defense contractors and researchers and road builders. There's a myriad of interest groups, corporations, unions, professional groups, constituents, and colleagues, all of whom want just that one little bit of the federal dollar, and who can make an eloquent case about how what may benefit them personally will also benefit the nation as a whole.

There's nothing sinister or malicious about any of this. In a sense, this is how the process of government works: out of the clamor of different voices and divergent needs, we forge policy and a sense of direction. But I remember often sitting in those meetings and wondering, "Who speaks for the common good? Who stands apart from this agitated group of special-interest people and thinks about the good of the country?" This is not, by the way, a new question. Thomas Jefferson, in his first inaugural address, urged Americans "to unite in common efforts for the common good."[4] And those who make policy, the Founders thought, should maintain a "disinterested attachment to the public good, exclusive and independent of all private and selfish interest."[5] The Founders spent a lot of time pondering ways to encourage this, and the system they came up with—separating the government into three, co-equal branches—was designed with that goal in mind. Thinking about the good of the country, in other words, is the job of the Congress no less than that of the president and the Supreme Court. All too often, though, Congress has fallen short.

There is no single force to blame for this. The high-stakes gamesmanship of politics today, the influence of campaign money, the sophisticated strategies of lobbyists, the growing complexity and scope of legislation, the sheer demands on the time and energy of members of Congress, the extraordinary diversity of the American people—all make it difficult for an individual member of Congress to step back and sort through what he or she believes is right for the country. And why do so when you don't need to? Please enough self-interested groups, and you've hammered together a majority. That's considered to be realistic congressional politics these days, and there are those who argue that it's the way things ought to be: everybody working for his or her own self-interest, they argue, is what makes this country work.

But I don't think that's what Jefferson and others had in mind. Seeking to please as many groups as possible may be how you gain or hold on to power, but it is not how you govern wisely. I can't help but think that the remedy for much of what ails our political system is for each of us—ordinary citizen and member of Congress alike—to restore in our lives a sense of the public good, to ask ourselves not what's good for any one of us, but what's good for the country. That lies at the very heart of a well-functioning, strengthened Congress.

Just recently, I've seen stirrings of this on Capitol Hill: members who have been willing to set partisan or personal considerations aside and work together on the desperate economic straits facing the country; members who have launched new policy initiatives they believe can address problems that weaken us as a nation; members who have made clear they take seriously the role that strong oversight of the executive branch can play in keeping the federal government on track. It is all a reminder that Congress is in many ways a living institution, evolving as politics, the American people, and the times demand. It has had its ups and downs over the years, sometimes fulfilling the role the Founders envisioned for it, sometimes falling well short of the mark. I believe we stand at the brink of an era when Congress can, if it wants, rebuild its standing in the constitutional firmament. I hope it does, for our nation can only benefit from a Congress that reasserts its prerogatives and lives up to the faith our democracy places in it.

Appendix 1

How to Judge Congress

There are several things to look for when trying to judge whether Congress is a strong, well-functioning institution. Each year at the end of the session, the Center on Congress at Indiana University asks fifty leading political scientists from across the country to evaluate Congress on how well it did over the previous twelve months. We look at more than twenty key measures, not just one or two. And we do this less to point the finger of blame than to find areas in which Congress can and should do better in the future. These are the questions we ask:

1. Does Congress protect its powers from presidential encroachment?
2. Does it carry out effective oversight of the president and executive branch?
3. Does Congress generally fulfill its national policy-making responsibilities?
4. Does Congress allow members in the minority to play a role?
5. Does Congress follow good process and conduct its business in a deliberate way?
6. Does it engage in productive discussion and allow all points of view to be heard?
7. Does the legislative process involve a proper level of compromise, consensus?
8. Does Congress keep excessive partisanship in check?
9. Is the congressional leadership effective?
10. Does Congress hold members to high standards of ethical conduct?
11. Does it focus on the key issues facing the country?
12. Do members educate themselves well on the key issues facing the country?
13. Does Congress consider the long-term implications of policy issues, not just the short-term?
14. Does conflict in Congress reflect substantive differences, rather than political game-playing?

15. Does Congress do a good job in passing the federal budget?
16. Does Congress reflect our nation's diversity?
17. Does Congress make its workings and activities open to the public?
18. Do legislators broadly reflect the interests of their constituents?
19. Do legislators make a good effort to educate their constituents about Congress?
20. Do legislators make a good effort to be accessible to their constituents?
21. Does Congress keep the role of special interests within proper bounds?
22. Does Congress reform itself sufficiently to keep up with changing needs?
23. All things considered, how well does Congress represent the American people?

So there's a lot to look at when you are trying to judge Congress.

But there's more to this than just evaluating Congress. We also ask the experts to evaluate *citizens*, to judge whether they are doing their part to make our system of government work well. We ask how they would grade citizens on—

1. Contacting their members of Congress on issues that concern them?
2. Following what is going on in Congress on a regular basis?
3. Voting in congressional elections?
4. Working through groups that share their interests to influence Congress?
5. Understanding the main features of Congress and how it works?
6. Having a reasonable understanding of what Congress can and should do?

How would you do on these six measures? The political scientists have been tough graders of both Congress and citizens.

(For the results of our latest survey, go to the Center on Congress website at www.centeroncongress.org.)

Appendix 2

Analyzing Congressional Arguments

If you are trying to become more engaged in the work of Congress and would like to follow better what your legislator is saying, it helps to understand the basics of an argument presented by a member of Congress. Whether made on the House or Senate floor, in a press release on a website, or in a local public meeting back home, the member's arguments will typically involve several of the following components:

1. *Facts and figures:* At the core of a legislator's argument are the main facts about the issue and some key figures. These are the foundation upon which all else is built—the percentage of people in poverty, the number of business failures, or a list of key natural resources in a particular region of the country.

2. *Examples and illustrations:* Specific examples can help personalize the issue, going beyond facts and figures to make the discussion more concrete and connect it to real people—which in the end is what the work of Congress is about. For example, a legislator might recount a conversation with someone who was struggling to make ends meet, having to choose between home heating oil and health care.

3. *Effectiveness of solution:* Congress passes legislation to do something, to accomplish something, to address a particular problem. So members try to indicate why their proposal will be effective—for example, that a proposed tax break to encourage the development of alternative energy sources will actually work, rather than just waste the taxpayers' money.

4. *Historical understanding:* The issues before Congress don't just arise in a vacuum. Usually there is a long history of legislation in a particular issue area. So members will often place a proposal in historical context—for example, looking at how well a similar measure previously passed by Congress worked out.

5. *Connection to core values:* It helps to connect a proposal to core values shared by Americans, such as how it will promote equal opportunity, protect individual liberty, strengthen the family, help hardworking people get ahead, or make America less dependent on other countries.

6. *Fairness:* Fairness is a major consideration—Americans are uncomfortable when a proposal hurts one group to help another, or provides benefits to one group while excluding another group with the same need. Members of Congress know they will hear protests from their constituents when they think a bill would treat them unfairly.

7. *Long-term consequences:* Many of the proposals before Congress have an immediate impact, but they need to be helpful—or at least not be harmful—to our country in the long term. If someone proposes an extra benefit for retirees on Social Security, what are the long-term cost implications and how much of a burden will be placed on today's younger workers to pay for it over coming decades?

8. *Comparison to alternatives:* In Congress there are almost always different, competing proposals for how to solve a particular problem. So legislators will try to argue not just that their idea is a good one, but that it is better than the main alternatives.

9. *Anticipated objections:* Arguments are stronger if they can anticipate major objections and respond to them in advance. So a significant portion of a member's statement will often be devoted to responding to possible criticisms by opponents.

10. *Opinion of experts:* The issues before Congress can be complicated and technical, and cover an incredibly wide range of subjects. So legislators do pay attention to the opinion of experts. Thus it helps to be able to point out what some recognized experts in the field have to say about the proposal.

11. *Public support:* Members of Congress are elected to represent the interests of people back home. So it strengthens their hand if they are able to point to surveys indicating that a large percentage of the public supports action on a particular problem.

12. *Political support:* How many other members of Congress support the proposal (particularly people from both parties)? What about the congressional leadership, party leaders, the administration? What about major interest groups, like the Sierra Club, the National Association of Manufacturers, or the League of Women Voters? The greater the political support, the better.

13. *Emotional component:* Legislators can't base their entire case on emotion, but it is not irrelevant in motivating colleagues to vote for a proposal. So a floor statement by a member of Congress will often go beyond a simple list of facts to stir up emotions as a way of heightening the case they are trying to build. Members can feel passionately about the issue they are discussing, and it often shows.

So listen carefully; see how many of these you can spot; and then evaluate how convincing they were.

Appendix 3

Twelve Ways to Contact Your Member of Congress

You've decided to get in touch with your member of Congress about an issue that matters to you or your family. That's great. But don't limit your approach. There are many ways to reach him or her and to make your voice heard. Here are twelve:

1. *Send a letter:* The traditional way of advising your representative or senator of your views. Members of Congress typically give high priority to responding to letters from constituents, and you will almost certainly receive a response.

2. *Send an e-mail:* This is now by far the most popular way of contacting members of Congress. As long as you are e-mailing your representatives (rather than sending a blanket e-mail to members all across the country), it will generally receive the same attention as a letter.

3. *Sign or initiate a petition:* This lets your legislator know that several people feel the same way you do.

4. *Call on the phone:* Call either the member's Washington, D.C., or the local office back in his or her district. You can't count on getting through to the member, but you can certainly pass on a message. And most members do set aside some time to call back constituents.

5. *Meet with them in their Washington, D.C., office:* Members' D.C. schedules are generally quite tight, but they will do their best to step out of a meeting to talk to visitors from back home. You may end up meeting with your member's staff assistants, but they are often quite knowledgeable in specific issue areas.

6. *Meet in their home office:* It is easier, and often more productive, to schedule a meeting back home, away from the distractions of the Capitol. Personal contacts like this are particularly effective.

7. *Participate in local town meetings:* Members regularly hold public meetings when they are in their districts. Look for the schedule on your member's website, and don't hesitate to speak up.

8. *Participate in online, virtual forums:* Many members of Congress now hold "virtual forums," similar to town hall meetings but done online. You might find this an easy and convenient way to participate in discussions with your legislator.

9. *Invite him or her to speak to your group:* You can ask your member of Congress to meet with your local or neighborhood group. This is a good way to start a dialogue, and there is strength in numbers.

10. *Participate in conference calls:* Members of Congress are increasingly reaching out to constituents via conference calls. Check with his or her office to see if one is planned sometime soon, and join in.

11. *Respond to a survey:* Many members will send out surveys—by mail or online—to solicit the views of their constituents on issues before Congress. Fill one out and add any other comments or questions you might have.

12. *Meet with his or her staff assistants:* Each member of Congress has district representatives, legislative assistants, caseworkers, project managers, and others who are excellent points of contact. Schedule some time to meet with them.

The key is finding the approach that works best for you. And keep in mind that effort pays off. If you can do more than one of these, that's even better.

The best way to find the contact information for your member of Congress—mailing address, phone number, e-mail, and the like—is online. You can get to his or her congressional website through www.house.gov or www.senate.gov.

Appendix 4

Making Your Case Effectively: Some Do's and Don'ts

Whatever your reason for getting in touch with your member of Congress—whether you are concerned about a national issue like health care or energy policy or a local one like a new road in your community—you will make more headway if you follow a few basic do's and don'ts.

Be factual: Do become knowledgeable about the main facts on the issue, so you are able to make your case with facts, not slogans or rhetoric.

Be clear and concise: Do make your case briefly, because there are many demands on a legislator's time. Stick to one or two issues rather than nine or ten.

Be personal: Do go beyond generalities to explain how an issue will affect you and your family personally.

Be inclusive: Do state who else supports what you have to say, such as others in your church group, labor union, or community board.

Be constructive: Don't just point to problems, but try to find ways that they can be constructively solved.

Be informed about Congress: Do take time to understand the basics about Congress and how it works.

Be a listener: Do listen carefully, to better understand how your legislator's thinking is developing and what sorts of considerations would influence his or her final decision.

Be courteous: Even if you disagree with your representative, don't get upset, raise your voice, or make threats. Stick up for your views, but in a civil way.

Be aware of the rules: There are strict limits on what legislators can receive from someone trying to influence them. Don't bring expensive gifts or promise campaign contributions. Know the rules and follow them.

Be open to compromise: Don't expect to get everything you want. Recognize that legitimate points can be made on the other side, and that the final bill will likely reflect some degree of compromise and accommodation.

Be patient: Don't always expect to get an immediate commitment one way or the other. Many issues are complex and demand time for deliberation and consultation.

Be persistent: Do follow up after your initial contact. Keep in mind that legislators hear from a very wide range of people on a large number of issues.

Enjoy yourself: Finally, relax. Don't worry about making the perfect presentation or writing the perfect letter. Say what you have to say, and enjoy your exchange with your representative in Congress.

Notes

1. Why We Need to Restore Power to Congress

1. Dick Cheney, interview with Bob Woodward, *Inside the Presidency* (PBS, January 21, 2005).

2. James Madison, Federalist No. 49, February 2, 1788, *The Federalist Papers* (Library of Congress). Available online at http://thomas.loc.gov/home/histdox/fedpapers.html (accessed February 14, 2009).

3. Sandy Streeter, *The Congressional Appropriations Process: An Introduction* (Washington, D.C.: Government Printing Office, February 22, 2007).

4. Robert Kaiser, "Congress-s-s-s; That Giant Hissing Sound You Hear Is Capitol Hill Giving Up Its Clout," *Washington Post*, March 14, 2004, final edition, p. B01.

5. Woodrow Wilson, *The President of the United States* (New York: Harper & Bros., 1916), p. 51.

6. Alexander Hamilton, Federalist No. 70, March 15, 1788, *The Federalist Papers* (Library of Congress). Available online at http://thomas.loc.gov/home/histdox/fedpapers.html (accessed February 14, 2009).

2. A Stronger Voice

1. David Baumann, "King of the Budget," *National Journal* 37, no. 7 (February 12, 2005): 456–461.

2. Michael F. Cannon, "An Unhealthy Tradition: Medicare Miscalculations," *National Review* (March 26, 2004).

3. Robert Kaiser, "Congress-s-s-s; That Giant Hissing Sound You Hear Is Capitol Hill Giving Up Its Clout," *Washington Post*, March 14, 2004, final edition, p. B01.

3. Strengthening Congressional Oversight

1. Kirk Victor, "The Inability or Unwillingness of Congress to Make Thorough Use of Its Oversight Powers to Keep the Executive Branch in Check," *National Journal* 36, no. 2 (January 10, 2004): 104.

2. John Adams and Charles Francis Adams, *The Works of John Adams, Second President of the United States: With a Life of the Author, Notes and Illustrations* (Boston: Little, Brown, and Co., 1865), p. 462.

3. Carl Hulse and Christopher Marquis, "The Struggle for Iraq: Congress, G.O.P. Split over Inquiry on Prisoner Abuse," *New York Times,* May 19, 2004, p. A1.

4. Dan Kennedy, "The Big Story," *Boston Phoenix,* May 21, 2004.

4. Restoring the Deliberative Process

1. Norman J. Ornstein, "Don't Sacrifice Deliberation for Expediency," *Roll Call,* July 9, 2003. Available online at http://aeipress.com/publications/pubID.17953,filter.all/pub_detail.asp (accessed February 15, 2009).

2. David Corn, "Foreclosure Phil: Would You Trust the Man Who Broke America's Financial System to Fix It? John McCain Does," *Mother Jones* 33, no. 4 (July 1, 2008): 41.

3. Scott Lilly, "When Congress Acts in the Dark of Night, Everyone Loses," *Roll Call,* December 6, 2004. Available online at http://www.americanprogress.org/issues/2004/12/congressdark.html (accessed February 15, 2009).

4. Gary Mucciaroni and Paul J. Quirk, *Deliberative Choices: Debating Public Policy in Congress* (Chicago: University of Chicago Press, 2006), p. 200.

5. Ibid., p. 197.

6. Ceci Connolly and Mike Allen, "Medicare Drug Benefit May Cost $1.2 Trillion," *Washington Post,* February 9, 2005, final edition, p. A01.

7. Norman J. Ornstein, "Debate over Motion to Recommit about Norms, Not Rules," *Roll Call,* April 18, 2007. Available online at https://www.aei.org/publications/filter.social,pubID.25975/pub_detail.asp (accessed February 15, 2009).

5. Reducing Excessive Partisanship

1. Jeffrey M. Jones, "Perceived Inaction Largely behind Low Ratings of Congress," *Gallup News Service,* September 5, 2007. See also "2007 Political Scientists Survey," *The Center on Congress,* January 16, 2008. Available online at http://congress.indiana.edu/learn_about/feature/survey_political_scientists_dec_2007.php (accessed February 15, 2009).

6. Strengthening Ethics Enforcement

1. James Wilson and Bird Wilson, *The Works of the Honourable James Wilson, L.L.D.,* vol. 1 (Philadelphia, 1804), p. 145.

2. John R. Hibbing and Elizabeth Theiss-Morse, *Congress as Public Enemy* (New York: Cambridge University Press, 1995) and *Stealth Democracy: American's Beliefs about How Government Should Work* (New York: Cambridge University Press, 2002).

3. "2008 Public Opinion Survey Overview," March 2008 Survey, The Center on Congress, June 27, 2008. Available online at http://congress.indiana.edu/learn_about/feature/survey_public_attitudes_march_2008.php (accessed February 15, 2009).

4. William Branigin, "Democrats Take Majority in House; Pelosi Poised to Become Speaker," *Washington Post,* November 8, 2006. Available online at http://www.washingtonpost.com/wp-dyn/content/article/2006/11/07/AR2006110700473.html (accessed February 15, 2009).

5. Thomas E. Mann, "An Independent Entity for the House Ethics Process?" Testimony before U.S. House of Representatives Task Force on Ethics Enforcement, April 19, 2007.

7. Curbing the Influence of Lobbyists

1. "2008 Public Opinion Survey Overview," October 2008 Survey, The Center on Congress, December 12, 2008. Available online at http://congress.indiana.edu/learn_about/feature/survey_public_attitudes_october_2008.php (accessed February 15, 2009).

2. Robert J. Samuelson, "Lobbying Is Democracy in Action," *Newsweek,* December 22, 2008.

3. "Lobbyists Double Spending in Six Years," April 7, 2005, The Center for Public Integrity (www.publicintegrity.org). Available online at http://www.democratic underground.com/discuss/duboard.php?az=view_all&address=132x1738775 (accessed March 6, 2009).

4. Donald L. Barlett and James B. Steele, "How the Little Guy Gets Crunched," *Time,* February 7, 2000.

8. Strengthening Citizen Participation

1. Adlai Stevenson, "The Educated Citizen," speech given at Princeton University, Princeton, N.J., March 22, 1954. Available online at http://infoshare1.princeton.edu/libraries/firestone/rbsc/mudd/online_ex/stevenson/adlai1954.html (accessed February 15, 2009).

2. Constitution of the Commonwealth of Massachusetts, June 15, 1780. Chapter V, Section II.

3. Robert A. Katzmann, *Daniel Patrick Moynihan: The Intellectual in Public Life,* 2nd ed. (Baltimore, Md.: Johns Hopkins University Press, 2004), p. xx.

4. Thomas Jefferson, Letter to Charles Yancey, January 6, 1816, in *The Works of Thomas Jefferson,* Federal Edition, 12 vols., collected and edited by Paul Leicester Ford (New York: G. P. Putnam's Sons, 1904), vol. 11, p. 497.

5. James Madison, *The Writings of James Madison,* vol. 5, 1787–1790, edited by Gaillard Hunt (New York: G. P. Putnam's Sons, 1904), p. 223.

6. Bernard Bailyn, *Faces of Revolution: Personalities and Themes in the Struggle for American Independence* (New York: Knopf, 1990), p. 267.

9. A Well-Functioning Congress

1. Arthur M. Schlesinger, Jr., *The Cycles of American History* (New York: Houghton Mifflin Harcourt, 1999), p. 274.

2. "11 Issues for the Next President," *Congressional Quarterly,* October 6, 2008, p. 2647.

3. Paul C. Light, *Government's Greatest Achievements: From Civil Rights to Homeland Security* (Washington, D.C.: Brookings Institution Press, 2002), p. 46.

4. Stephen Browne, *Jefferson's Call for Nationhood: The First Inaugural Address* (College Station: Texas A&M University Press, 2003), p. 36.

5. Carter Braxton, quoted in Gordon S. Wood, *The Creation of the American Republic, 1776–1787* (Chapel Hill: University of North Carolina Press, 1998), p. 96.

Index

Lee H. Hamilton is Director of the Center on Congress at Indiana University, a nonpartisan educational institution seeking to improve the public understanding of Congress and encourage civic engagement. From 1965 to 1999 he served Indiana in the U.S. House of Representatives, where he was chairman of the Committee on Foreign Affairs and the Permanent Select Committee on Intelligence. Currently he is President and Director of the Woodrow Wilson International Center for Scholars in Washington, D.C. Hamilton was co-chairman of the Iraq Study Group and vice chairman of the National Commission on Terrorist Attacks upon the United States (the 9/11 Commission). He is author of *How Congress Works and Why You Should Care* (Indiana University Press, 2004), author (with James A. Baker) of *The Iraq Study Group Report,* and editor (with Thomas H. Kean) of *The 9/11 Commission Report.*